World
Peace?

Preface, January 2003,
page iii

"Letter to an Islamic Fundamentalist",
March 1993, page ix

World Peace?, 1983, page 1

Supplement, 1985, page 116

Anthony J. Donovan
New York

Cover photo is courtesy of NASA.

For information:
A. Donovan
120 East 4th Street, #1 B
New York, NY 10003
antoneD@aol.com

This edition printed by
BooksJustBooks.com

Additional design by
BudgetBookDesign.com

Library of Congress Catalog Number: 86-71893

ISBN: 0-9617258-0-X

PREFACE

The call: Genuine relationship.

Despite decades of concern and discussion, I find it helpful to remind myself how very little I know.

This I believe: The only possible way to have security among nations and peoples is to have strong alliances, strong, personal healthy relationships. Trust only comes with continued effort, experience and sincerity. Leadership has more to do with service, clarity, and the inner struggle to gain insight into underlying conditions and emotion than bravado. Security does not come from arrogance or rhetoric, the fine sounding but insincere and empty language without verifiable deeds.

Our life we share on this planet is extremely precarious, vulnerable and precious. Since childhood we've seen bravado too often as the face covering our underlying insecurity and fear. It can also be the mask of malfeasance and malevolence. But it is a learned response when integrity seems threatened, and the leader of the most powerful nation on the earth has recently bolstered its use. The only silver lining of 9/11 was the opportunity of having the world together on the same page at the same moment. Inexperience let too much of that good will dissipate.

One of the earth's great ongoing battles is between truth and deception. My experience of when the truth is uttered, it is not arrogant, but oft stark nakedly clear and humble.

-O-

The United States remains the great new global experiment. While we know and accept there has to be moderations with our civil liberties presently, I stress presently, if we lose them over a long term, we lose what the world admires about us, and much of what America stands for and what millions died for. We lose our forefathers vision and life's dedication. The world is still watching.

-O-

"Terrorism" was a frequent headline in 1983. Gorbachev hadn't arrived yet. President Reagan was calling the USSR the "Evil Empire" while several in our government were attempting ways to get the UN out of the country. NYC Mayor Koch had just called the UN "a cesspool". Leaders of states in different blocs were not yet talking to each other, even behind closed doors. The tension and mistrust in the hallways was so tense and palpable, I could not use a tape recorder or even the names of most for their fear of being associated with unofficial comments. The world began changing. By 1985 diplomats in *World Peace?* could at least be acknowledged.

The books relevance was reborn for me when recalling two decades ago such vivid scenes as the Afghani representative pleading for us to understand that the so-called "freedom fighters" the US government were supporting wanted to destroy everything we valued too. More chickens back to roost.

World Peace? was the result of a personal search, not connected with the UN, or any governmental, political, religious or social group. Simplicity is its strength. The paths to solutions then remain the same paths today, with only slightly new twists.

-O-

Long term solutions remain in the realm of winning peoples hearts and minds. They remain in consensus building and spreading those international norms and values which prevent and disallow acts of hatred toward religion, race, philosophy, gender, nationality.

iv

Around the world all speak of the desperate need to create jobs, of meaningful livelihood. That's the world's task; to create jobs around our needs; to apply ourselves fully, guide and transform these global challenges, mainly our military industrial complexes toward international security and global solutions. The world yearns for the unscripted inspiration and leadership that can refocus our efforts towards this.

There are some significant additional challenges to those listed in 1983, which call our tremendous energy and creativity to the table: economics, the gap between rich and poor is growing shamelessly; the extreme degradation of poverty breeds yet more dangerous hatred and ignorance; sheltered corporate greed and malfeasance remains too often unchecked and without restitution; over population especially in poverty areas expanding; city congestion rising, including needs for transportation infrastructure and livable space; homeless shelters and prisons over full capacity; a congested and backlogged system of justice;

Spin, spam, false advertising, child sex trades, illegal, lethal and misinformation in telecommunications; both free and controlled media that often misinforms and too narrowly represents; lack of education, educators, and resources for educators; air and water pollution rising; quality of food compromised; dwindling of natural resources, while the need for them and energy increases; threatening atmosphere and climate changes influencing further draughts floods and famines; great natural and human treasures lack protection; diminishing essential forests, wetlands, and fertile seabeds; slave trades continue to exist, and slave labor being used; great epidemic diseases continue; medicines and medical care are largely unaffordable; international law and basic human rights remain unknown of in some parts of the world and disregarded in others; sense of genuine participation and voice in "democracies" are challenged; small and large crime and extortion rings pray on the desperate around the globe; black markets of the most horrific and destructive materials known and unknown to most humanity available now to any individual or group; terrorist cells further entrenched; international arms industry continues to impoverish by using up the majority of worlds GNP; although there is reform there still is no international body trusted to have teeth and go up against one of the countries with veto power in the Security Council if ever need be, and the cycle of resentment, vengeance and competition for influence continues; and space, it's resources and scientific discoveries remains largely untapped.

-O-

Space exploration is vital for human progress and possible survival. It's funding is often questioned, and dwarfed by small military budgets. It is an area that answers our creative and adventurous spirit. We don't know which generation will need knowledge of space to survive or deter an arriving meteor or drastic change in atmosphere from a yet unknown influence. There are infinite discoveries that have been and will be beneficial to us. Someday one could answer our energy needs by harnessing the suns vast energy and beam it down to earth.

We do not need a large meteor to be on our path, or another world war, or nuclear holocaust to make us realize our commonality. Poverty, greed, injustice, and hatred remain common enemies to turn around and make good on.

-O-

Without naiveté about real threats, the trillions being spent on creating walls, fences, and guarding extensive boarders makes better sense to go towards investing in and nurturing relationships with our neighbors where mutual cooperation, security and trade are a common necessity and goal. For us that means further embracing and trading with Mexico and Canada.

Nationalism, national cultures and even corporate cultures now, need continual integration with the whole. The answer can't be who can wave their flag most visibly and intensely, for the North Koreans would have us all beat. There is only one country in the world where every citizen appears to agree with it leader, and that is North Korea. The suffering to keep it that way is incalculable, and no resources can sustain it over time.

-O-

The life threatening matter of "non-interference in internal affairs" still smoke screens and allows large debilitating human atrocities and genocides. Gathering an understanding that we can and must strengthen international law and an international body that can face and deal with this issue is essential for all the listed reasons, but especially because; the unspeakable horrific deadly materials of one renegade can be made, kept and sold anywhere and everywhere; because corporate malfeasance can and does live anywhere and everywhere and at times absconds with hard earned monies of others without reprisal; because sound global economics need global ground rules; because crime rings know no boundaries and live anywhere and everywhere; because inhuman atrocities anywhere degrade humanity everywhere; because one nation or one group of nations acting alone perpetuates the cycle of distrust or vengeance; and most of all, because all the common challenges we face above need each of us everywhere to be part of the solution.

Non-interference allowed inhumanity to continue from time immemorial. Not including the devastating world wars, in our recent century we saw vast unspeakable internal horrors as they rolled into each other, from Turkey's genocide of the Armenians, to Germany's final solution, Stalin's purges, Mao's cultural revolution and China's "liberation" of Tibet, our cold war played out in Vietnam, Cambodia's abandoned to cleansing, South and Central American death squads, Uganda, Burma, Somalia, Bosnia, Rwanda, Sudan,

East Timor ... it tragically goes on. We have all played some part, but the point is to move on toward future solutions. Again, this can be stopped in our dawning millennium through an efficient, cooperative international mechanism.

-O-

While welcoming and embracing the Chinese people as all others, I remain concerned with their government continuing to be the chief proponent of "non interference." In these last several years that the US remains the single greatest economic strength it would strongly behoove us to champion a solid international structure so when China takes over the leading economic role, there will be a sound counterbalance to their fervent ethnocentricity.

The nation or group with the most money will have the newest, smartest, and most destructive weapons in the future. When the toothbrush, the TV, computers, most gizmos, shoes and clothes we are wearing and soon cars are mostly made in China, one doesn't need to be an economist to discern who will someday have power be able to do what they wish, like us recently. One doesn't need to be a historian or ethicist to know that this "most favored nation" continues to and has severely violated human rights, destroyed whole cultures in our lifetime, covers up and holds hostage innumerable measures by disallowing any mention or process of dialogue about these matters. Again, we have to win hearts and minds.

-O-

A world committed to protecting the weak everywhere is preventative medicine and the one Achilles heel of terrorism. It's my hope that war for the common good will emerge someday only as an international endeavor and duty, forever keeping in mind President Carter's testimony, "War is sometimes a necessary evil, but it is always an evil." Yes, in extreme cases it is necessary. Avoidance of war, and avoidance of inhumanity, can well lead to far greater evil and eventually wider war. If war is the world's duty for the greater good, may it be swift, carried forward with dispassionate wisdom, and as careful and respectful of all life as possible.

-O-

I recently was walking atop small grass covered mounds surrounded by silence that once were great walls and buildings of the flourishing cosmopolitan city of Ani. For hundreds of years it rivaled the power and influence of Constantinople. As they once did, we often think our cities can live forever. Including the vast measures being put in place today, the greatest walls constructed for protection, stone or paper, ever built by civilization after civilization have all crumbled or been rendered useless in time. What used to take many years and large armies, can now take just a handful of misguided ideologues to walk around. Leadership. Hearts and minds. Dialogue. Relationship. Education.

-O-

What we learn on a personal and family level applies universally; somewhere, at some time, forgiveness will have to factor in. Not forgetfulness, or avoidance, but the inner learning of forgiveness. I know of no one way to get there. None of us have been perfect. It's recognizing our wrongs, not dismissing them, and moving forward from here. With tragic scars and imperfect results, what seemed impossible between the US and an USSR, and in a divided Northern Ireland, South Africa, Lebanon, the Balkans and East Timor there now shine a few of the positive examples that this struggle to end hatred, along with the support of international concern, does both bear fruit, and a better world make.

I believe in prevention, and hope each of us are guided

in our choice to make the world in front of us a better place today. Humans have a great capacity for higher aspects of fulfillment and relationship. It often takes tremendous courage to be here. May we embrace our duties, blessings, and love in life. During this profound occasion of transition, may *World Peace?* lend useful encouragement and hope.

January 22nd, 2003
New York City

MY LETTER
TO AN ISLAMIC FUNDAMENTALIST

"My Letter to an Islamic Fundamentalist" was sent out to various home and overseas Arab newspapers a week after the 1993 World Trade Center bombing, and printed by two soon after 9/11. The opening phrase is the opening phrase of many passages in the Koran. My letter was more innocent, geared to those who continued to contemplate blowing up life and my home. We know more now that it is not only injustice and poverty that brings us "terrorism". Along with our other fundamentalists "Islamic fundamentalists" are not to be equated with being "terrorists". Unchanged, the letter was, and remains a plea for dialogue.

In the Name of God, the Compassionate, the Merciful.

We know little of each other. I do know that our Christian and Jewish "fundamentalists" here in America think, as I hear you do, that much in the world is going astray, not living up to the law of God, and that "Satan" is running rampant and must be fought against. Seeing the vast amount of man made suffering, I can agree with much of this.

We in the West are told the majority of you have little in life; That you have not been given access to education, nor proper health care; That you are not politically represented, or listened too. We understand that you have been repressed by many regimes over the years, which has included torture, imprisonment and death; That you share many hardships economically; And that while many of you are in this oppression of poverty, you have found the strength of each other, and the strength in common faith. Your clerics have reminded you, as our priests, ministers and rabbis have, of your worth in the eyes of God, and each other.

We hear that the Mosques have often helped provide essential community health care, food, and shelter, where the state was negligent. Repression, oppression and lack of representation are worth getting radical about. The founders of the United States of America did in the 1700's. There are some aspects of your passion and conviction that we need reminding of in ourselves, and in which we would greatly gain from, in correcting our own social and political ills, and maintaining vigilance with our own hard earned Declaration of Independence, Constitution and Bill of Rights.

I read much of the Koran a few years back. There are many beautiful and inspiring passages, and passages that we all in the world can benefit from. There are several references supporting the fact that Christians, Jews and Muslims worship the same God, and that we share many of the same prophets and their messages. I was however, often made aware by the strong "we/they" language and that because I may not be living by every precept, or that I was not a confirmed Muslim, that I was an "infidel", an unbeliever. As you know, the Koran has very little to say about infidels that is nice. As a matter of fact, the Book tells you often that infidels are what is wrong with the world. It tells you that we are often evil itself, the bearers and cause of sin and injustice. Some passages encourage you to rid the world of infidels, and that in the eyes of God we deserve to die.

Scholars have a field day with all of our sacred books. There is language in them all which support a compassionate, caring and loving life of service, and language which also encourages us to judge, divide, and destroy those who do not believe as we do. Unfortunately, none of our rabbis, ministers, priests, or clerics singly possess God's overview, and all knowing, and as a result some of them have misused their own limited understanding and interpretations of the "Word of God" to the detriment of a world of God, in my limited opinion. Very few will tell you or I, that there is no guaranteed copyright to the pure light of God owned by anyone. On the contrary, many will tell you they have it.

I have no doubt, and many here in America are aware now, that we along with several other countries supported some regimes in the Middle East that have been cruel, arrogant and unjust. And we did support these regimes often for our own resource needs. But what most Americans were not aware of, was the price many of you had to personally pay. I genuinely apologize for our part in this suffering, large or small, but it will take more than that.

Americans for the most part see themselves as a God loving country. We see ourselves as compassionate, as being for the underdog, the poor, the lonely, the unfortunate. These are many of the people who came to build America, and they haven't forgotten from where they struggled. But yes, along with our charitable ways there is arrogance, greed and selfishness among us.

Greed is a human element that is hard to keep in check. We do have laws and do put people in jail if they are caught stealing or making unlawful profit from others. However, greed and selfishness, two tools of Satan as the Koran says, are not solely with us in the West. I have traveled to the Middle East and other country's with large Muslim populations. I have seen Muslims here and abroad just as caught up in the symbols of greed, in limousines, in big houses with servants, and with the most fashionable and expensive jewelry and clothes, or arrogantly treating others inferiorly. I personally don't see having wealth as wrong, unless those individuals are not engaged somehow in making life better for others. This quality of soul is impossible to know from a passing limousine, or by the clothes one wears.

You yourself know how hard it is to be a saint, a perfectly holy Muslim. If you have gotten to know those among you, and even your loved ones in your family, you must have witnessed hypocrisy, and transgressions from "God's law". Having done some soul searching of myself through the years, I am aware of the hypocrisy at times in my own thoughts. And I imagine, we being both humans, that you have similar inner struggles at times between what you are told is correct and what you feel to be correct, or between what you believe is right and what you actually do in every instance.

I can assure you that most of the people that I know in America are very respectful of others, of themselves, and of God. They believe that material things are not what is most important in life. They would be upset if they found out something they or their country were doing was harmful to others in anyway.

As you feel, many of us feel strong in righteousness. We think of ourselves as trying to help people in the world, and as people who try to relieve suffering when we see it. We will stand for good morals and for what we think is right and just. The problem lies in that neither you nor we have all the facts. We are both fed stereotypes and propaganda which antagonize, create and exacerbate our divisions.

Our press and yours have bias. They both have a strong proclivity to label. That makes things only seem easier to understand, more black and white. For you, any attack by "the Great Satan" is against all of Islam. For us, any bombing by "Islamic fundamentalists" is an attack by terrorists trying to bring down all the goodness that our society is worth. Please know that in both our lands this simplistic labeling is the irresponsibility of the press and politicians, and those few among us who stand to profit from divisions, fear and war. These people often do not share your moral committment, nor your moral courage to sacrifice your lives for the larger truth, God's truth.

Most citizens are horrified at the loss of life. And especially at the loss of innocent life, of women and children, and unarmed working civilians. It is true that America really came to action only when our access to oil was threatened, and Kuwait was run over by Saddam Hussein after our years of supporting him. I readily admit oil is not the most noble of reasons to go to war. But what really horrified us, and I would assume would horrify you if you knew the details, and made us especially regret not following through with Saddam's removal, is when we people found out that the person we had been supporting for years was murdering his own, executing any political rivals and those not agreeing with him. We are now finally admitting to and getting the evidence of him and his Baath Party killing over 100,000 Kurds in the north; men, women and children of all ages. Here, the man should lose all credibility with both you and us. Mass executions of the innocent can never be God's work, and claiming to be God's servant makes this worse.

He does this in the name of Islam. This confuses us. It must also confuse you when we say we are Christians and believe in brotherly love, and yet you hear about CIA assassination plots, our bombs blowing up hospitals and orphanages, and you hear that money and wealth in our society is our prime motivator, something we idolize. From my perspective you see a life terribly distorted by our own advertising business. It is mostly hype, and twists the reality that the majority of us toil and live in. We have come to know this ourselves, but you may not know this. It is true that sex, wealth and violence attract people's attention, but the vast majority of us live modest, simpler lives. Most of us work hard and pay heavy taxes, much of which go to social programs, but yes, more goes to the military. And yes, we along with many other nations are still suppling deadly armaments around the world, which in my eyes, is feeding Satan's fires of intolerance, of might is right, of communicating to our fellow human beings with guns and death, rather than the basic human interaction of listening and talking.

And yes, it is true, you are correct, even though many in our government have lobbied for a stronger international response, we have been too slow to act in Bosnia. The whole international community can feel shame in not protecting the innocent from this unchecked horror. The international process still lacks maturity, and the will. We need not take sides, but we certainly must all be in the business of protecting the innocent from such cruelty.

I consider myself a radical fundamentalist when it comes to the point of knowing that we can live in better harmony together. I know we can. I believe this deeply and fundamentally from my own experience. I know that we can develop a better knowledge of each other, and that we don't have to kill, or oppress each other. I believe we are more alike than different, especially now that we can look down from space upon our one precious planet.

Our great Holy Books can be used to guide and inspire

us towards a better life. But these same books can be used by some of our preachers to divide us, and create suspicion. I have listened and had my heart warmed and my mind stirred to positive human action by Rabbis in a Synagogue, by Priests in a Church, by Gurus in an Ashram, by Chiefs in an Indian ceremony, Lamas in a Temple, and by Clerics in a Mosque. But unfortunately all too often, what I consider a common human limitation comes up. Eventually, I have heard in each of these settings a spokesperson bring up a "fact" that this particular path is the only true path.

It is this one sentiment, fueled by strong need for assurance and an identity, that leads us to distrust each other. The one and only true path language attempts to make us completely right, by others being completely wrong, and leads us to separating each other in our hearts and minds from the human family.

The wise ones of all religions know all about the human family. I have been in hospitals, clinics, and schools run by Muslim Charities, by Jewish and Christian Charities. There is a tremendous amount of sacrifice, generosity and kindness put forth by our better aspirants in the service of God through their faith, and for humanity.

One good thing about our country is I can never assume that I am speaking for anyone else, certainly not for the country. Probably much like you, I gather my information from those I'm in contact with. I have my friends. I have my relatives. I have my work, and I read the newspapers. Even my closest relatives can argue with many of my cherished thoughts, so I don't expect less from you or anyone else in the world. Luckily, I have traveled in many different countries, and live in a city where I have been required in my tasks to interact with all colors, and nationalities and religions. This has helped me see through the false stereotypes and labels put on all of us. I have found myself "at home" in the homes of Muslims, Christians, and Jews alike. I have witnessed friendly spirit, respect, and a kind, generous hospitality in each home, sometimes in different ways, but none more, or less than the other.

Many of the "Western Values" that you want to protect yourselves and your children from, are the same characteristics of society that many of our parents make efforts to shield their children from, i.e. violence, unchecked lust, prejudice, and greedy, selfish life styles. Don't think that because Madonna posters sell all around the world that we don't know the difference between image and reality, or that we all listen to the same music. When thinking of art, I would like to read someday more of the Arabic manuscripts. For me, it remains the most beautiful writing among all others.

"Satan" is a reality to some, and a concept to others, but for both, "Satan" is something we each have to struggle with in our own selves. Satan doesn't like Christians, Jews, Buddhists, Hindu's or Muslims any more or less than the other. When a hard working, God fearing American wakes his children up in the morning and reads in the news that a bomb has killed innocent people doing their daily work, to him this is Satan's work. To your radical element this same bombing is God's work and the people who planted the bomb are "soldiers of God, martyr's for the cause".

When our military fires rockets to destroy a military command center that is believed to be planning and supporting executions and assassinations, it is seen as a tough measure, but is done with much of the same strong sense of righteous duty. Of course, if you or your fellow countrymen are on the other side of this attack, and especially if a rocket has gone off course and killed innocent people, this attack is the work of "Great Satan". I personally would like this cycle to end, for you and me. I am not alone.

I know that if the only way to stop you from harming my children was to kill you, I would. And I know you would do the same to me. We both have courage, and uprightness. God is on the side of the righteous, and we both feel very righteous in protecting the innocent and the poor. But we both must know that there are people among us that are cowardly. To me there is little bravery in planting a bomb, and there is even less bravery in pointing a rocket on a computer screen. I don't think either person is assured a place in

Heaven for their work. I think the real courageous work of healing and building a more caring world is what we will be judged by. And we both view ourselves as doing that. We both need to know who the enemy around us is; lies, greed, poverty and a hateful heart. There is none of God's love, compassion and mercy in us when we hate.

I would also ask you not to assume that the people you are told who are at the center of evil, those who work in the institutions on Wall Street, or in the big banks, don't have consciences, that they don't have family values, or a belief in God. I am sure there are a number of people that don't have these values, as with anywhere in the world, but I know many who do share these values and live for them. I know because I have some family members who work and make a living in these institutions.

In ending, let me say I would like us to join hands and gather our forces to end oppression throughout the world. If I may pray out loud: Let us together renounce the torture and killing. Let us stand up against wrong, whether it is in our own land or anothers. Let us respect each other's differences and individual needs. Let us support our common humanity. Let us not be fooled by words, by slogans or by images, but let us find the reality behind all the propaganda and rhetoric we are each bombarded with. Let us work cooperatively to end poverty. Let us face together the larger problems and challenges that make our streets unsafe for our children and elderly. Let us pray to God together that we do God's good work here on earth.

When we meet in that mutual respect, know you are most welcome in my home.

Most Sincerely,

Anthony J. Donovan
March 1993

World Peace?

A work based on interviews with foreign diplomats

Anthony J. Donovan
New York

Grateful Acknowledgement
to my parents, each of whose character and love inspire me onward. To three dear friends; Celia Thorpe Candlin for her wording corrections on a few passages she read, Maxine Lieghton for getting some of this on computer, Ralph Haarup for the cover layout work. I cannot acknoledge enough, God's grace all along the way.

And Deep Gratitude
to the following diplomats who responded and took the time to sit with me. They made this possible. To each I am indebted. Seeing their names here together displays the reality of diversity and unity among mankind:

Second Secretary Mr. Abdul Weedy, Minister Counsellor Abdelouahab Abada, Attache Mr. Jeronimo Gaspar de Almeida, Ambassador Lloydston Jacobs, First Secretary Sr. Rogelio Pfirter, Second Secretary Mr. John Thwaites, Counsellor Mrs. Eva Nowotny, Counsellor Mr. Rahim, First Secretary M. Johan Swinnen, Consulate Mrs. Marie Valgas, Attache Mr. Borio, First Secretary Mr. Rudolph Yossiphov, Second Secretary Mr. Aung Swe, Counsellor Dr. Jose Luis Jesus, First Secretary Sr. Raimundo Gonzalez, First Secretary Mr. Chin Yung-tsien, Ambassador H.E. Sra Emilia Castro de Barish, Counsellor Dr. Carlos Acero-Montejo, Attache Mr. Milan Kavarik, First Secretary M. Tep Khunnal, First Secretary Mr. Kristian Hojersholt, Counsellor Mr. Ronald Shillingford, Counsellor Sr. Luis Vidal, Counsellor Dr. Ali Rahman Rahmy, Attache M. Denys Krynen, Attache Mr. Schutze, Counsellor Ms. Uta-Maria Mayer-Schalburg, Second Secretary Mr. Devine Kwapong, Attache Mr. Ametrecopoulas, Counsellor Dr. Ferenc Somogyi, First Secretary Mr. Amitav Banerji, Counsellor Mr. Anin Riamom, Attache Mr. Assadi, Second Secretary Ms. Pauline Conway, Attache Mr. Uval Gat, Second Secretary Mr. Tsuneshige Iiyama, Counsellor M. Norbert Rakomalala, First Secretary Mr. Keshav Raj Jha, Ambassador H.E. Fafowora, Counsellor Mr. Ryszard Krystosik, Attache Mr. J. G. Eiselen, Attache Mr. Jimenez, First Secretary Mr. Kobsak Chutikul, Counsellor M. Coawovi Gogo Germa, Second Secretary Mr. Vefahan Ocak, Attache Mr. Nikita Smidovich, Counsellor Bui Xuan Ninh, First Secretary M. Nguyen An.

With special thanks to H.E. Ambassador Zenon Rossides for allowing me to use some of his published statments and for his and his wifes', Mrs. Theresa Rossides, continued friendship and reinforcement in the reality of "the moral flow of the Universe."

Dedicated to
my friend, Maureen Cotter
who pushed aside the darkness to care for and serve others,
and with her natural zest, faced both her life and death
with great courage.

and to
my brother, J. Timothy Donovan
for his honest and pioneering spirit,
who has carried a sense of responsibility, justice,
and understanding with all of the earths' people.
A companion, who throughout life has exemplified
true brotherhood.

and to
You, the reader, and all humans
who are daily doing their best in small as well as
great ways to bring light, truth, compassion and a sense
of belonging to our fellow inhabitants of this beautiful,
yet burdened world.

Note to the reader

This work does not pretend to have all the answers, or questions. There are no famous personalities interviewed, but highly qualified people. Nor is there any flashy news breaking story, yet the work of these men and women actually help to save our world on a daily basis.

I would be most content if readers said "there is nothing new to me here." That would strengthen my faith in this world. My one wish is that this effort wouldn't be necessary.

When talking about the sometimes rather amorphous word, peace, it is perhaps easier to follow with writing an amorphous book. I hope this is more than that. There is repitition, words and themes heard frequently, but by different voices. If fifty people are identifying a common solution, problem or idea it sometimes cannot be echoed enough. There is some redundancy as each chapter is meant to stand by itself and the subjects overlap.

One warning is that the diplomats are given open platform here. Truthfulness was incouraged, however, if the South African delegate says there can be room for us all, if from Iran we hear we are living by God's law, if Afganistan says the people want the Soviet troops there, if China points to U.S. and U.S.S.R. hegemony without looking at their action with Tibet, if Vietnam says it is in Kampuchea to help the people, if the U.S.S.R. says it is only building arms to catch up and protect itself from an aggressive U.S., and on and on from all nations, then it is left for you to use your own good discernment of truth. This work could not possibly cover worthy criticism, analysis, and cross examination of all the issues rendered by each diplomat. That was not the goal or intention offered in this rounding.

The purpose of this work is to however humbly and modestly, increase the possibility of a safer world; allow some vent for overwhelming pressures; and to help decrease fear which leads to war, terrorism, and the expenditure of vast human and earthly resources used in the name of security and defense throughout the globe, against one another.

Communication being a key in facing mankinds challenges, my objective was to get some questions straight, to converse genuinely and clearly, and to move yet closer to common understanding. It was to simplify and to help us see through the propaganda and rhetoric that all nations and people partake in. This was not always achievable.

These words are presented in the hopes of furthering trust. It is not for speed reading, rather weighing and reflecting on individual statements, passages, and chapters. "World Peace" was written in the mood of the interviews -- contemplative.

For me it is not a finished work, not an end, but another beginning, another attempt. Thankyou for participating.

The interviews began in January, 1983. This book was completed Thanksgiving, 1985.

Contents

INTRODUCTION

Terrorism has been on the rise. There are over forty countries engaged in war. Expansive debts threaten the world economies. There are several civil wars. Armaments are increasing in sales and use, and there is a heightening of tension, rhetoric and propaganda in the international arena.

International interdependency is now reality and the major saving grace for each country on this one globe is cooperative and clear communication.

For this purpose the author sat individually with ambassadors and/or appointed delegates from foreign lands with the intent that they contemplate and search themselves on five basic issues in need of clarification.

Each was asked about the meaning, to them, of a much misused word today, "peace", and world peace. Further, they were asked:

What are the major problems in the world today, the root causes of the multiple conflicts?

Do they see solutions?

Share thought on the escalating arms race.

Comment on the effectiveness of the United Nations -- an institution formed by world powers, including all the earth's nations with a goal of promoting world peace.

From where do they derive inspiration?

The names of the diplomats were not used to encourage a frankness which could free them from their nation's jargon, if they chose, and provide a safety. Because of his age, vast experience and personal effort with this topic, the 91-year old Honorable Ambassador Zenon G. Rossides of Cyprus, the last interview, is an exception.

FOREWORD

When Mahatma Gandhi arrived in India from South Africa he was asked to take on the task of leading his country out of it's turmoil. He replied, "...But, I do not know India." And so, the next several months were spent traveling throughout his land .observing, talking with the people, feeling out the issues, educating himself and taking notes. He knew, only a well informed conscience can make a balanced action.

To understand what can be done to make a better world, many of us do not have the means or time to travel to each country -- there are now over 160. However, resources are here in New York City. Although there is debate over it's effectiveness, the United Nations is the largest international resource center, the single most inclusive international forum, the gathering arena of all the earth's nations and their representatives. It is comprised of men and women whose life work it is to know, present, and defend their nations' interests in view of the whole. In the face of an often overwhelming sense of futility they are involving themselves daily in the process of cooperation, and in finding the mutual ground upon which relationship with each nation on this planet becomes possible. Despite the rhetoric, the propaganda, the bureaucracy, the superpower veto control, the loyalties, the special interest groups, the blocs, the power games, the individual ego imbalances and the cocktail parties, the United Nations embodies a vast wealth of experience and well-weathered work, tapped into here in this contemplation and search for ways to world peace.

World Peace is talked of in most every diplomatic speech. All heads of state say they want it. If you go to any international conference anywhere these words are repeated in almost every other paragraph, year after year. Hence, the question arises: Where are we going wrong? What is happening? Is anyone listening? Here is an attempt to seek answers.

One of the great believers in a United Nations never got to see it manifest. Franklin Roosevelt wrote these words on the last day of his life.

> The work, my friends, is peace; more than an end of this war -- an end to the beginning of all wars; ...as we go forward toward the greatest contribution that any generation of human beings can make in this world -- the contribution of lasting peace -- I ask you to keep your faith. The only limit to our realization of tomorrow will be our doubts of today. Let us move forward with a strong and active faith.

In joining hands with that faith, three major themes, among others, were most often repeated in these interviews: first, strengthen the structure of international cooperation and collective security, the United Nations, as intended by it's founders; second, improve the quality of communication; third, in trade and exchange continue working towards a more favorable global economic structure.

The Celebration of the Fortieth Anniversary of the United Nations in October and the Geneva Conference of November, 1985 are in part a confirmation of the hopes and convictions expressed within this work. These face to face meetings of leaders of states linked with good will and the person to person human contact begin to address the call of those interviewed and the billions of people on earth.

A DEFINITION OF WORLD PEACE

"Morality is the basis of things, and truth is the substance of morality. Truth is my sole objective...and my definition of it has been ever widening."
                    Mahatma Gandhi

"My House shall be called a house of prayer
for all peoples."
                    Isaiah

One of the objectives of this work was to see if we all were talking about the same thing when we said "peace" or further, "world peace". When one listens to official speeches from every country, from every diplomat, one hears the word peace constantly. Without exception all say they want it, and most say it is because of some other nation that they don't have it. If everyone wants it then why are there so many wars being waged? Are we talking about the same goal? Does the word mean the same?

The word is overused, highly politicized, and often simply misused, as a tool in propaganda. But what was hopeful was that in these interviews each diplomat, from Russia to Argentina, from Madagascar to Denmark, from India to Costa Rica, showed a genuine concern and dedication to it's unfoldment. There was general agreement on a basic meaning of world peace. Each used often the exact same words in defining the term. The word has been bantered around so much that its translation into all languages, through all customs, through all lands, through all philosophies, has spread to a shared sense, a shared meaning.

This has been a major first step in a long journey. Next must come the constant vigilance, work, toil, and life-force to continue the shared perception. To this end many diplomats talked of peace as not being a passive term. It requires dynamic, active, often courageous effort, and has more to do with tolerance, patience, true strength, and inspired leadership. The earth is not in a condition where world peace exists or will exist unless there is a great deal of earnest care given.

The following are words diplomats used in defining and describing peace, world peace. In this chapter the names of each of the quoted nations are left out to help sense the unity of this voice. How to carry these words through is dealt with in other chapters. As one diplomat stated, "...Yes, but we are not angels."

Granted, each of us defines the world with our own senses, experience, and conditioning. Webster's Dictionary defines the word "world": "the earth and its inhabitants, with all their affairs and interests; hence, humanity; mankind..."

There are infinite personal interpretations of the word peace. Here are a mere few meanings from Random House Dictionary: "...To become reconciled; a state of mutual harmony between people and groups; to end hostilities and abstain from further fighting or antagonism; public order and security..."

The word most commonly used throughout the interviews in describing world peace was cooperation. For all it is very importantly the absence of war. For most it is more than that.

"It's freedom from colonial rule."

"Not only the absence of confrontation, but a friendly coexistence with our neighbors and all nations of the world."

"Peace is something relative. It is not only no war, but just as much being free of the tensions involved with the expectations of war."

"Being able to work for a living."

15

"To be able to live a normal life; to progress our standard of living; for our people to have the ability to work."

"I don't see peace as passive."

"Security, a neighborly feeling."

"A question of mentality, global mentality."

"It means doing something about the developing world."

"World peace means resolving differences and not bringing force into play."

"Peace is the survival of the economy. Trade."

"Equitable trading.... It is respecting others' points of view."

"Absence of tensions and threats. A sense of understanding that the resources of the globe belong to all nations and not any one. Peace is a sense of justice." [Justice is another word commonly used.]

"Easy to say, but difficult to define. It should have a deeper significance, a deeper individual understanding. It has much to do with tolerance, an extension of non-violence. We have an ancient saying: The world is a family."

"We don't define it. We feel it."

"Peace means to be friendly, to love life, to be interested in living."

"World peace means listening to others, trying to achieve the goal of common understanding."

"Only by this cooperation can we avoid disaster. Not a question of ideology, but a question of survival."

"Allowing people to fulfill their destiny. The people taking power and effecting change."

"Peace means no more countries divided by wars, no more families divided."

"Peace doesn't flow out of the end of a barrel."

16

"Peace means having conditions under which we can develop, and have our basic rights insured."

"Respecting human rights."

"Peace is the advancement of development and civilization for all mankind, for the whole earth's peoples."

"World peace involves allowing others to develop as they need and respecting their own internal affairs."

"We need it."

"World peace is defined in the five principles of non-alignment; non-interference, respect of national sovereignty, peaceful coexistence, non-use of force, and against the politics of blocs."

"It's an idealistic concept. ...I am a believer in the basic principle that there is room for all of us."

"Peace is when His law is implemented. When there is justice in the world, there is peace. Peace is the principle. War is the exception, the aberration."

"It is the objective to which we are committed."

"It's not quite feasible, but something to aim for."

"Exchange. Exchange of tourism, culture, education, goods, etc." [Exchange is often used.]

"Peace means to live and let live. Love others as you love yourself. Giving each other the opportunity to raise our children. Peace means giving me some quiet life. To be able to stop for coffee in Syria, Jordan, Lebanon, Israel, and Egypt."

"We want to achieve good. You must work very hard for peace." "Peace has never been in general. There are constantly conflicts in the world. World peace means doing something to resolve them."

"World peace is a process. It's better life. It would be like a large musical concert."

"It's my belief; peace of mind. It is, if people can realize their aspirations."

"It is reconstructing our country. It's independence and liberty; friendly relations with all."

"It is acceptance of reality, and acceptance of limitations; seeing room for improving; a condition of objectivity."

"Even in view of all the catastrophes all through life, there are pockets of peace through it all. Peace is everywhere. It is our own concept, based solely on faith. I don't know if there is any broad based scheme which can bring about peace. It is something the individual must achieve. The concept of peace should not be limiting, surface or shallow, but deep within the individual."

Yes, and the list can go on. What is important here is that these are words you or I could say. They are words that you may think come from your country, but they come from all the countries -- "hostile, opposing, enemy", as well as "friendly". So, the diplomats all want world peace. With the many tongues there is a familiar voice.

MAJOR WORLD PROBLEMS

"Peace to have meaning for many who have known only suffering in both peace and war, must be translated into bread or rice, shelter, health and education, as well as freedom and human dignity."
Under his portrait at the United Nations,
Ralph Bunche

"...Learn to love the questions themselves,... live the questions now. Perhaps you will then gradually, ...live along ...into the answer."
Rainer M. Rilke

Terrorism is most often a desperate act born out of desperate circumstances, and usually effects those not responsible or even connected to the problem. Terrorism is not something new, and yes, we can join together and do something about it. It is like a cancer surfacing on the skin which must be attended to carefully and quickly. However, the deeper, the root cancer lies beneath this symptom. As stated by several delegates, the world today faces political, economic, and moral crises. And in this we are all inextricably linked, a shared responsibility.

Every country has it's own multiple problems. Most like to point the finger elsewhere, until in the final analysis we have come full circle in accusations. If we can get to the core of problems, if we can understand what they are, we begin to get glimpses of the inherent solutions. The tremendous complexities surrounding all the issues often wear down on the willingness, patience, endurance and courage needed to face them. In unifying to solve problems we benefit by first knowing what they are. The following paragraphs will attempt only to list the major problems confronting nations, and peoples today. Do not get discouraged.

"Poverty is the main problem." "The colonized countries have been sucked dry." "People don't have the means to live. There are dictators. U.S. citizens would not tolerate it either." "There are major refugee problems here." "We are all the way down now. There is no money." "Hunger." "Everyone wants control. If they own anything they are afraid of losing it." "We have to import most of our products. Our production is low. We are in an undeclared war. Anything we build gets destroyed. Many of our professionals have left."

"War is ruining our economy." "The border is uncontrollable." "Several countries are forming a union against us." "U.S. imperialism." "Soviet expansionism." "Chinese expansionism." "Vietnam's invasion and colonizing of us." "Turkey's invasion and colonizing." [etc. on the invasions]

"Our land was bombed 200 days and nights in 1973.... We worked the people too hard. There was much anger and killing. We lacked communication. We were in a strong position so we didn't want to talk at the agreements. We now recognize this as a big mistake." "They took over our country, in the name of liberating us."

"It's not a question of optimism or pessimism. The world is completely different today. Now we are all confronted with several crises."

"The Soviets cut relations with us in 1967." "The U.S. severed relations with us."

"Now our people are too highly politicized. People are from the far left or the far right. There is a feeling of general discomfort.... Still some families own most of the power. Economics everyday are getting worse. The black market is a strong group."

"Our problem is that we live at the border of two ideologies which oppose. These ideologies are behind most of the wars today." "I don't know if these countries want peace."

"Some countries are in desperate shape. They need food immediately." "Our problems are the same for all undeveloped countries; lack of industry, no technology, difficult financial constraints, and high unemployment. Many of the people migrate to other lands for work." "There is overpopulation and resulting deforestation." "There is drought and desertification. Agriculture is very low." "Developing countries know what they want. Our [developed country] goals are not as clearly defined."

[All countries spoke of the economic problems.] "That country is the largest recipient of U.N. aid, yet opts for a welfare system and continues to have a declining gross national product (GNP)." "Give us a chance to sell our products. The more people are out of work, the more they are idle. From that, problems arise." "If there isn't help to pay the extreme debts, it will be the collapse of the monetary system." "The major problem for all developing countries is the economy. Insurgency problems are related to this as well as black markets and drug trafficking."

"We are poor. We have a large amount of people and our natural resources are low. The present economic structuring is not in our favor. The price of our exports are going down and the price of imports are going up." "The western market builds resentment when it fixes our prices and tells us how to control our raw materials." "We allowed many immigrants into our country. But they keep to themselves and do not mix with us. They are now taking over many of the businesses. This creates much internal tension."

"We haven't been politically stable. Terrorism has been a problem. We are trying to find a way of reducing internal economic tension."

"The major problem is the global economic deterioration. There is a maladjustment of trade. New York and Washington dictate the prices of commodities." "The Economic Council of Developing Countries (ECDC) has improved south-south negotiations, but we need help from the World Bank which is controlled by the west." "Developing countries are often not developing. They are financially getting worse. There is a resource and brain drain to the west" (or north).

"This overwhelming debt may cause military threats." "Security has a more economic and social base."

"The major problem is economic. Much of which had to with our being in a state of war for thirty years and the military spending. Also the growth of population has contributed to the crisis." "The world economy is structured in a way that we have low wages and high tariffs imposed upon us." "The present tendency of the great powers is protectionalism in terms of trade. Labor, not goods, is cheaper in developing countries." "We are trying to meet the balance of payments but our economy is in stagnation." "Political and economic problems are always combined."

[There are many comments on communication] "Claiming this country to be in your own backyard is self-serving and egocentric." "Presently the north-south dialogue is poor." "A language of condemnation is often used towards one country to get support from others." "Much of what is done here is in the name of peace but not from the source of peace. There are gaps in understanding." "Media plays a tremendous role, but is often not objective." "I see many hard times ahead for there is a general climate of distrust." "We are used as a focus and scapegoat. There are atrocities of much greater magnitude in other countries which are ignored in comparison."

"The north is not convinced of the concept of interdependence. They will not recognize that their destinies are linked with the small nations of the south. How can we

24

have good educated positions for dialogue if these realities are hidden? We can't."

"We are not good speakers. Our language and customs are quite different."

"The major problem is the deterioration of the language of politics." "The heightening of rhetoric is a threat to peace. Rhetoric masks many issues." "Strong idealism anywhere can be self-deceiving." "Some less stable countries resort to war to generate a national unity." "As long as there is a tendency to categorize you won't have peace." "Ideology is a problem. It is hard to get through it to see what is really happening with the people. Ideology is often a pretext for ambitions." "There is a separation of speech and reality; a form of self-intoxification by politicians."

"We wish to open other exchange but if our country is linked with either the U.S. or the U.S.S.R. then the other country will not negotiate." "We depend on dialogue between the U.S. and U.S.S.R. and feel pressures coming from both sides. They don't communicate with each other." "There is a deliberate attempt by the developing countries to focus on the east-west confrontation."

"Both the U.S. and U.S.S.R. [etc.] deny being aggressors, yet we must look at their deeds." "Russia is misunderstood." "The West is misunderstood." "The major threat is the growing tension in the international climate. The spiralling arms race can be extremely dangerous."

"The United Nations Charter has been breached time and time again. We have moved far away from the charter. The U.N. needs strengthening." "Every small country needs to be aligned with a superpower." [The U.N. cannot protect them.]

"The problems lie in the fundamental difference between the approach of the western world and the eastern. It is democracy, freedom of speech, press, artistic endeavors, and

private enterprise against it's opposite and serving the state."
"Tensions arise with governments who do not put people
first. It's man a tool of the state, versus the state existing for
man." "The super powers have their own aims and neither
are prepared to abandon them." "The main problem is the
rivalry of the two superpowers. They have interests all over
the world. They both feel threatened and both claim to be
safeguarding world peace."

"The arms race and the arming of small nations is the
major threat to peace." "The international tensions pull
nations towards defense and away from development." "The
framework of international relations is confrontation and there
is intercontinental bribery." "We are witnessing the decline of
old structures of control and we don't know what they are
being replaced by yet. We fear it, but let's not hide it." "We
can't have world peace with the concept from the middle ages
of the nation states."

"Like most people everywhere, the people here mainly
care about their own lives, not international concerns."
"People have stood up before, but they were killed. People
think it is better safe and alive." "Those who have, wish to
keep the status quo and don't want to take political or
economic risks."

[A pressing problem for many nations is the fact that they
are engaged in the devastation of war.] "We have taken in
many thousands of refugees and now our border is being
invaded because they say we are 'helping the rebels.'"
"These countries' aim is our destruction." "One-fifth of our
population and 60% of our wealth was destroyed by the
war." "No one can claim total victory in this region. It is a
matter of saving face."

"The selling of arms to our neighbor has hurt the
sentiment between our two countries." "We don't want
military bases here and be a future battlefield." "The arms
race has already been transferred to space. Many satellites
have military purposes."

26

"Our people are now disillusioned with the new revolutionary governments. There were many promises, but reality has been one terror story after another."

"The problems are passion, greed, and violence in the self. Peace will take time because these elements have become institutionalized, often not even subtly." "There is too much turmoil in general, even within the basic family structure." "Give us a chance to sell our products. The more people are out or work, the more they are idle. From that, problems arise." "I cannot understand why in this very well-off country there can be so many in need."

"We all say we are here for peace, but the more one gets involved, the ways to achieve peace become less evident."

And so there are infinite problems facing us all: food shortages, natural disasters, terrorism, rhetoric and propaganda in common language, lies, population growth, drug trafficking, organized crime, bureaucratic corruption, wars, opposing military alliances, militarizing space, atmospheric pollution, chemical and radiation leaks and accidents, ecological disregard as in toxic waste dumping and deforestation, endangerment of our natural habits and wildlife, poor sanitation and contamination of vital water supplies, epidemic disease, drought, desertification, mass starvation, tides of refugees, non-communication, political and economic blocs, east-west, north-south, Marxism vs. capitalism, developed-underdeveloped, systemized repression, unbenign dictators, invading and colonizing countries, lack of representation of minorities (and sometimes majorities) throughout the world, aggression, greed, superiority-inferiority, putting the blame elsewhere, the irresponsible use of democracy or socialism, human rights abuses, uncared for, unguided, unprotected children throughout the earth, the stifling debt, trade imbalances, lack of unified vision, and with it all a crippled United Nations Security Council unable to implement its decisions.

As intricate as this list is it is not complete. Each country has its own internal geological, political, social, economic complexities to be added. Individual countries were not cited above with each phrase because almost every statement forms a part of all of our problems. No one nation can solve the above alone. Each country can either help or hinder the process of facing each problem, together. For this reason we need a true United Nations, a more effectively functioning world body.

SOLUTIONS
FOR A MORE HARMONIOUS WORLD

"To be a philosopher is not merely to have subtle thoughts,
nor even to found a school,
but so to love wisdom
and to live accordingly to it's dictates,
a life of simplicity, independence, magnanimity,
and trust.
It is to solve some of the problems of life,
not only theoretically
but practically."

Henry Thoreau

"Realistic, comprehensively responsible, omnisystem-
considerate, unselfish thinking on the part of humans does
absolutely effect human destiny.   ..., then the
accomplishment of that realistic conceptioning is realistically
effective in satisfying [the] Universe [and the] human mind is
accomplishing its designed evolutionary role."

Coiner of the phrase "spaceship earth",
Buckminster Fuller

There is no one solution. When problems are many and complex they demand the solutions which match and reflect these complexities fully and comprehensively. We are beings and nations in process. We are moving toward the answers when we take the first step of becoming aware of the problems. Then must come the will to give what is required in the task, great or small, for as Albert Einstein said: "A problem cannot be solved at the same level of consciousness it was made." Solutions are inherent in the problem. When found, then comes their delicate and vital dissemination.

It would be easier if there were just good and bad, or simply the have and the have nots, simplifications which many rhetorically call "reality", but the issues are in shades of gray, not black and white. Solutions have many ingredients, the major one being communication. They require work, courage, a sense of justice for all involved, tolerance, will and an ability to listen, among other things. In today's rapidly moving world, as one hears voices from around the globe, it becomes evident that only in co-existence can there be any existence for us all.

It is tragically unhealthy to our international integrity when proposals are not listened to, nor accepted or rejected on their own worth and merit, but because they come from a particular country or bloc.

Poor or unbalanced solutions only create worse problems for the future. None of us can know enough. We are all growing and learning together. Ultimately our security will not lie with U.S. security or U.S.S.R. security, but in a true international security as the U.N. Charter called for and has yet to realize. People must be fed, listened to and communicated with sincerely, as we become increasingly aware of our collective vulnerability.

Each head of state and each government adds or detracts from the process. But perhaps most important is the fact that each human on the earth makes a difference and affects the shaping of our shared future. It is this collective mind of individuals throughout the globe which can raise the veil of destruction and allow yet another new dawn for mankind.

From one who warned us of a rising military-industrial complex, President Dwight D. Eisenhower: "I like to believe that people in the long run are going to do more to promote peace than governments. Indeed, I think that people want peace so much that one of these days governments had better get out of the way and let them have it." It is this reason that the members of these governments were approached as individuals, as people, involved in an institution which has yet to reach it's full effectiveness as peace keeper.

Standing on a battlefield site decades after World War II Dwight Eisenhower contemplated as any general from many a nation: "When I look at all these crosses.... Think of them. These men gave their lives in their prime so that there could be peace and freedom in the land, and put an end to war." We must think of them and the millions of civilians in less glorified graves.

From the ashes of these millions of soldiers and millions of innocent civilians was born the United Nations and the service it faces today. The wars and other acts of terrorism have not ended.

Here are a few words on approaching solutions.

"I'm optimistic. I think we can sort out the difficulties."

"Cambodian people must rule themselves." [This applies to all invaded lands: Afghanistan, Lebanon, Namibia, Tibet, Western Sahara are but a few.]

"We don't have much of a problem with world peace because we don't interfere with others' internal affairs."

"How can we then promote trust? Only through actual deeds, not words."

"Solutions? Yes, patience. Compromise, all the time. Any decisions must realize that others are involved."

"If the people are happy, this national resilience is our defense."

"We've learned that conflicts could not be solved by war. The scars are still open but we wish good relations now. Opening the dialogue is the best and only way."

"Since war is the first created in the minds of man, we put forward the idea of education of the young generation for peace."

"We claim to forget our past difficulties with each other. We wish to be friends."

"The rest of the countries need to be independent from and united in opposition to the great superpower rivalry. The U.N. should be strengthened."

"In my country there are two hundred different languages and customs. We are promoting good communication on the local level with every village. We see unity in diversity."

"Things can't get worse. We are condemned to agree. There is no more refuge."

"If you want peace in the world you have to be very active."

"We join no Blocs. If we join the East or the West then the other becomes an enemy."

"We hope there is a solution. If France and Germany did it, then we can. If you would have told me in 1976 that Sadat would come to Israel to make peace, I would say you are crazy. But he did."

"We've learned more [since Vietnam]. The people cannot be confused or fooled as easily about issues like in Central America now."

"If [X] country stops interfering, we would like to be on more friendly terms."

"We believe in the step-by-step approach. Every country needs to make a little contribution. Each country has a role to play. It takes time. With each contribution it all adds up eventually."

"Exchange."

"In the long run, trade will help both parties."

"My country cannot exist without a policy of world peace. My country puts their trust in international mechanisms and law. We recently established a University of Peace."

"My country is connected by a thousand bonds to other countries. Half our income is realized through foreign trade. Most go to Socialist neighbors, but we've always maintained contact with capitalist countries."

"We have to share our technology with the third world."

"Stop fooling around with dropping a coin in a hat. Let's get down to business. Undeveloped countries need an economic base. The U.S. should get building industries with us."

"The U.S. and U.S.S.R. have direct responsibility for developing world affairs. They have the political and economic power and advantage. They have a direct effect as a whole."

"I've been here for several years and see clearly that no problem can be solved in isolation. The world is moving toward a shared responsibility. Governments need to listen to others and develop a feeling of self-containment. We need to accept differences."

"The best way to help ourselves is to help others."

"There needs to be a restructuring of the world economic order, and without jealousy."

"We need aid. People wish to keep the status quo. If we can only convince them that their quality of life will not worsen."

"The economic problem of the third world is great. Some say socialist is best and some say capitalist is best. They need to take an active part in developing themselves, but this can be solved only with cooperation by all countries."

"We need a sense of understanding that the resources of the globe and space belong to all nations, not to any one. The developed should assist the undeveloped. We need help with developing the sea bed, not just for our benefit but for all in trade. We need people to understand that we are a vital part of their existence, too."

"The total of the earth's problems may pull us together. The realization of the great extent of problems will hopefully lead to the emergence of a collective objective. My country supports the principles and functioning of the U.N. Charter."

"Solutions? First, realizing that we as humans and as spiritual beings have a common basis."

"Listen to others."

"It's a question of mentality, of global mentality."

"North [industrialized nations]-south dialogue and negotiations will contribute greatly to world peace. What happens in New York, Washington, and Moscow has a profound and direct effect on all nations."

"Let's sit and discuss."

"If you'll have good relations, you need to talk to and know your neighbors."

"If the two superpowers would only sit down and communicate and not send statements via the news."

"Keeping up the dialogue."

"Continual talks. We don't believe in revolution which destroys."

"We have good relations with the U.S. and U.S.S.R. We would react negatively to either side if they put a hand on us."

"We are a small country and bear in mind our limitation, but try to make our voice heard."

"After listening and carefully deciding, we follow through with our commitments 100%."

"In 1963 our first president envisioned a united Africa to balance out the powers. We need to change the economics around the exploitation of raw materials."

"Politicians need to expose themselves more and be real, allowing a vulnerability."

"The world needs a directed will; it needs leadership like King and Kennedy. I have faith and hope. I think leaders will come."

"The solution is for us to work, not to complain."

"We must have work for a living."

"We seek to diversify job opportunities. We want to develop relations with other islands. We're opening embassies in Africa and developing cultural exchange."

"We are no longer a big power. We've had to adapt to the world. It was understood that we had to transfer charge of colonized countries to a harmonious commonwealth composed of independent countries and based on mutual relations."

"It is my job to work and support the official role but world peace all happens and comes from the personal level."

"International security can only exist when the United Nations Security Council has the force called for in the charter to implement and back up it's decisions. Until this, terrorism and tyranny will prevail."

"One solution would be the gradual dissolution of the concept of nation states."

"Our people are very informed. You should come and see the mountains to feel the people."

"...to know something well means also to know the surroundings. It may be a method to study things alone, but no one can stop it at this stage. The final analysis must have the all taken into consideration. There needs to be firm conviction. There is a great need for global approach."

"We must strengthen the United Nations. ... We must go backand correct the original error [made by member countries] and follow the way outlined in the U.N. Charter."

"I am optimistic. With space there is a new impulse."

Space exploration will provide some new solutions and even more room for us in the adventurous and not so far off future if we can devote more of our resources to feeding ourselves and developing our potential today. The concepts we create and the technology we produce are only as good or bad (helpfull, humanitarian and creative or distructive and squandering) as we make them to be.

Terrorism is on the lips of all people today. War is certainly also terrorism. Terrorists fan their flames of violence by focussing on one country or one ideology as being the ultimate evil. This is convenient for rhetoric and propaganda. If there were an effective union of all countries, an effective union of force used in these situations, excluding countries directly involved, there could not be the idea of retaliation, not against 160 nations. But as long as one country or group has to fight, protect, and retaliate this cycle cannot be broken.

There are great hardships and injustices upon groups of people. These legitimate complaints are often the roots of terrorism. They must be brought forward to an international forum that also has some teeth behind it, in order to help alleviate and address the pressures. Otherwise, we will continue to see injustice met with injustice. There is, and has to be "room for all of us."

What can we, citizens of the world, do?

With limited ability, in humbleness I offer a few brief suggestions: We can continue informing and educating ourselves, realizing there is always another perspective, while widening our own sense of truth. Know that every voice counts and effects the whole of things eventually.

We need to sense what is behind words and power. Adolph Hitler rose to the highest level of destructiveness after convincing his people he would lead them out of their economic depression and political injustice. Communication remains the key, and there is much rhetoric and ideology for us to carefully sift through. Don't believe everything, but believe in something. Believe in yourself. Let us believe in an increasingly perfected and more effective United Nations.

For many of us there is the direct privilege of voting. Writing letters, sending telegrams, phoning our representatives all gets tallied and can make the difference.

Signing petitions, boycotting, and when necessary, nonviolent demonstrating and marching is vital. These are the tools of democracy. Help build or support the many local grass roots organizations and do-it-yourself self-sufficiencey projects. Plug into the networking on issues you believe in, or start the networking if it is not there.

While enjoying the wisdom and ways of our own individually rich heritage and dignity, embracing others strengthens us as a whole. We are all "foreigners", and all the "family of man."

Allow time for personal repose and nurturance, and time to feel our relatedness to, and responsibility for, the health of our universe, earth, nation, community, family and self.

Make time for a walk with nature. Have fun occasionally in song and dance.

In many traditional religious communities it is a wholesome practice to give part of our weekly earnings or time toward others, a worthy needfull cause, or charity. We are our brothers keepers.

Perhaps most important is keeping up our daily good work and life. Every true prayer helps, deepening our faith. Do whatever you think is necessary and helpful, on any level.

Gandhi's life and work, and the civil rights marches and war protests of the fifties onward inspired millions throughout the world. More recently, the anti-nuclear demonstration of June 12th, Live Aid, Hands Across America, and others are all positive and massive illustrations of individual people, not government, banning together to help, to raise consciousness and effect change.

Despite their present challenges, the election in the Philippines of Mrs. Aquino is a shining example to the world of the tremendous power people can generate when they use non-violent democratic means and get behind the cause of justice and integrity. The vigilance and work continues daily. Some things are worth dying for.

Let's remember the cruel and dehumanizing lessons of the past and present, and hinder their advancement. It takes one person to begin the ripples of hatred. It takes one person to begin to stop it and in so doing initiate positive life. One sincere smile, one outstretched hand, one lifted head goes further than meets the eye.

> "I thought to myself:...
> Somebody has to do something about this!
> Then I realized:...
> I am somebody."
> Senator Robert Kennedy

DISARMAMENT,
THE ARMS RACE

"Non violence is the only thing the atom bomb
cannot destroy."
                    Mahatma Gandhi

"They shall beat their swords into plowshares
and their spears into prunning hooks.
Nation shall not lift up sword against nation,
neither shall they learn war anymore."
                    Isaiah
        On a wall across from the UN

"It is not the power of weapons
but the power of spirit
that can save the world."
                    Zenon G. Rossides

The unleashed power of the atom has changed
everything save our modes of thinking, and thus
we drift to unparalleled catastrophe.

Albert Einstein

When a natural disaster strikes an area (hurricanes,
earthquakes, floods etc.) it does so to all people alike; white-
black, rich-poor, religious-atheist. Differences are dropped
for these few days or weeks as people pull together in their
momentary common vulnerability, common effort, and
common instinct to live and rebuild. They all work side-by-
side until danger is past -- a powerful reminder of our
common life here.

War and terrorism also pull people together.
Unfortunately though, it pulls people together to pull people
apart. It would merely be slightly better if only those wished
to be killed were killed, but in war and terrorism today it is
almost always thousands upon thousands of innocent, hard
working civilians who are humiliated, tortured, and killed.
Millions were coldly executed in Nazi camps; there are death
squads in Central America; Stalin scourged the people in

formation of his state; Nagasaki was not a military base, nor Dresden; there was China's Cultural Revolution, and the bloody takeover of Tibet and its' culture; there was genocide in Uganda; millions were executed in Cambodia; citizens missing in Chile and other countries; almost routine explosions in residential Beruit; children marched to their death in Iran; this list could go on and cover most peoples at one time or another. No land is free from the ability to commit atrocities or be "inhuman". Superpowers, bastions of ideology as they may be, hold the unleashed power capable of a destruction much worse than anyone's idea of inhuman atrocity.

It is only up to us, the people of the globe, to admit to such horror, denounce it, and take more responsibility for the course of our governments. Officials and soldiers just carry out orders, mechanically. This is their universal training, their duty and for them the only reality. If they receive the command there will be no contemplation if asked to shoot a gun, or push a button aimed towards New York, Moscow or Rome. It is done. Before long smaller nations will have access to this destruction.

If there would ever be survivors (documented as unlikely) there would be great lessons learned. A nuclear blast kills those labeled socialist or capitalist, and selfish gluttons or dedicated humanitarians alike. Those survivors would not care what religion, culture, skin, social structure or philosophy you have. It comes back to basics, the common struggle: Where do we find shelter? What can we eat? There will be unity in the mutual despair of losing all that you cherished and knew. In a recently found Brothers Grimm fairy tale is the story of a mother sending her daughter into the woods to save her from upcoming war. Even the woods or mountains cannot hide us today.

It is the author's belief that this horror will not happen and that we, people of all nations, have the ability to change our "modes of thinking".

Technology is a product of our great and creative mind. Technology is vital in our evolution, but it is as one wing of a bird. The other wing is our humaneness, our ethical and moral standards, our spirit. There is a call for balance. A bird cannot fly if one wing is larger than the other. With balanced wings we can explore, journey to and develop new worlds.

Bombs don't have such wings. Even the poisoning of arrows was considered very unethical in ancient Greece and therefore not used in combat. Nuclear weapons (the most sinister aspects of technology) are teaching us, and strongly encouraging us to upgrade and change our consciousness and ethical standards, or "we drift to unparalleled catastrophe". Each of us has a hand in creating this world.

Some questions on security: Have you ever felt the loud rumbling of tanks through your town during peacetime manuevers? How did you feel? Secure? Have you ever listened to survivors of Hiroshima or Nagasaki speaking about the ability to protect oneself? (And these were comparatively small detonations in contrast to the warheads today) Which gives you a more warm, secure feeling; watching seagulls gliding above in the blue, or hearing the thunder and seeing streaking fighter jets?

The following statements are not necessarily the official positions of the countries mentioned.

"The arms buildup is not a question of balance. Unfortunately, it's a question of superiority." (from Australia)

"We support every initiative for disarmament. It is very delicate. When the Soviets or the U.S. present resolutions we always vote for both, but often the resolutions are somewhat a pretense for their own interests." (from The Dominican Republic)

"We don't agree with the arms build up. It only increases the tensions, increases the suspicion and consumes [badly needed] resources." (Bangladesh)

"Globally, nuclear war is the main problem. We have initiated two documents for disarmament. We call for an approximate parody. Nothing can be gained by achieving superiority. The initiative lies within the U.S. and the U.S.S.R. more than the UN. The real situation is very complicated and must be taken in completely. Unless something is done, this will just get worse. Once it gets to space there will be further complications." [And it has already] (from Czechoslovakia)

"There is a nuclear imbalance in Europe. We have financed some U.S. missles. We have chemical weapons. We don't believe in unilateral disarmament. We have to work on it together." (from France)

"The first major imperative of the New Delhi Message (from the 101 non aligned nations) is disarmament; that is the non use of and the freezing of the production of nuclear weapons. Deterrence is an illusion, from the 19th century. Peace doesn't flow out of the end of a barrel." (from India)

"Armament is the third leg of our problems. For disarmament, the U.S. and U.S.S.R. need to work it out. I don't know if they will. If they don't what will happen is too ghastly to contemplate: world destruction." (from Nigeria)

"We understand the need for arms, for we were very close to the takeovers of Hungary in 1955 and Czschoslovakia in 1968. However, the present arms buildup is ridiculous. It doesn't lead to a balanced position when started in an inbalanced position." (from Austria)

"The arms buildup? No. The more arms, the more the tendency to use." (from Burma)

"We see all the military budgets to be directed to more beneficial, humanitarian projects." (from Egypt)

"War is first created in the minds of man. We put forward the Patsky Plan for a nuclear free zone in Central Europe and the education of the young generation for peace." (from Poland)

"We'd like to see both east and west pacts abolished. The Prime Minister has asked for the abolishing of the arms race." (from Greece)

"We are against nuclear arms and do not wish to be a battlefield or someone's umbrella. We don't want any foreign military bases." (from Indonesia)

"The arms race is inhuman. Balance is an illusion. They make more, we make more, until resources are totally depleted. Everyone is a loser." (from Iran)

"Each side says the other is in favor so we must catch up. This is not true. Talks should reduce results, yet, after each Geneva Conference there are always more arms produced." (from China)

"We import and produce armaments, but we are for total lateral disarmament." (from Brazil)

"We rely on international organization and law. Balance of power with armaments? How? It never ends." (from Costa Rica)

"Reduction in arms is the goal. Impossible to achieve, it seems." (from Argentina)

"Disarmament is often a theoretical problem for us, so we don't talk about it much. In Africa the problem is food." (from Algeria)

"Each general session we introduce new measures for disarmament. 1. Prevention of nuclear war, the crime against humanity. 2. Banning chemical weapons. 3. No space armaments." (from the U.S.S.R., presently innocent of the first)

"Your president "Ike" warned that the military industrial complex is too interested. But I believe that in the situation we have now, we are able to achieve an arms reduction." (from Bulgaria)

"It is important for the U.S. to have strong arms. But for the superpowers to be each spending billions is very sad." (from Dominica)

"Security has a more basic economic and social base, and not just a military one." (from Denmark)

"Development or armament, it is one or the other. You can't have both. We need to spend money on arms because of the aggressiveness of the world system. Not having the aid from those who have the means, many neighbors become afraid when the others buy arms." (from Cape Verde)

"The arms race is absurd. Why don't people see it as it is; a time bomb. When you see the U.S. (superpowers) with all it's potential, it is a pity. The impact is severe on the Third World. The percentage of resources being consumed is devastating. Here with all the unemployed, if there is no arms reduction there will be just more waste of resources, money, and time. Pakistan recently received 60 F16's (fighter planes) worth 3.2 billion and a green light to develop nuclearly. The expectation of war is almost as bad as war. It's a burden on ordinary people." (from Afghanistan)

"The history of mankind shows a ghost, war. But a nuclear war is very different. No one sees the arms buildup except the superpowers. In both hemisphere's the common thought of the people is against this. No one wants it. It is a lack of political decisiveness at top levels in both hemispheres." (from Columbia)

"We are human and of course, we don't like or believe in building war heads but....We are in a theatre of war with Russia on one side, the instable Iraq-Iran war on another, and our ancient enemy, Greece on the other." (from Turkey)

"I know U.S. companies in some business circles have a big interest in the arms race. They sell billions of arms to the world for profit." (from Vietnam, who received arms from China during war with the U.S. and up to the present is well armed from the Soviets. Commonly most nations have this need to get arms from one of the superpowers.)

"We are concerned about the Soviet presence in our region. We fear the introduction of sophisticated weapons. Disarmament is important. We need to spare our resources." (from Thailand)

"We are against the arms race. We are for equilibrium between the superpowers. In reality it may never happen. This is our goal. We are for the suppression of foreign forces in the Indian Ocean." (from Madagascar)

"If there is a real threat to world peace, the next world war would break out on our border. We want peace. We have to be armed to achieve peace. We believe in balance of nuclear power. We live so close to it. We need verification." (from The Federal Republic of Germany (West))

"The U.S. bases in Japan serve as a deterrent. The arms race is not ideal, but it is valid, a matter of fact. No one likes it as an eternal value. Without it how can we maintain this precarious balance? Sweden proposed a concept of cooperation, but how? There is no other alternative presently. A climate of trust and confidence must precede; without this, reduction is just idealistic propaganda." (from Japan)

"The world wants disarmament, but disarmament is impossible without international security." This, in a nutshell is what Hon. Ambassador Zenon Rossides of Cyprus has been saying in the UN since 1960. The clear headed veteran member of the UN has been a leader on the Committee for Disarmament but fears for the survival of this planet that too few are listening.

"Disarmament in itself is a negative concept. We will not halt the arms race by pretending that we are going to throw arms away. We cannot agree on parody. We can only be effective if we focus on a positive concept. International security is a positive concept."

And from his comments at the UN on October 18th, 1985 he continues, "To build collective security our primary concern should be to restore to the United Nations its intended effectiveness, as it was intended and meant to be under the Charter by its founders. The Charter bases itself on this security system. The principles of disarmament arise from that security system and are dependent on it.... In consequence of the failure to proceed toward international security, the structure of the world security has remained inoperable. Without a United Nations force there can be no way of enforcing the decisions of the Security Council. Therefore the decisions are ignored in the world and become mere pretense.

International security is the real problem, and not disarmament. International security is what we need to bring about for disarmament if it is ever brought about. So why do we (at the UN) forget all about it?"

From earlier statements, "We disagreed in 1946 over who would control the force, etc., but never tried to agree since. The five permanent member countries then agreed not to enforce article 43 of the Charter [which calls for the establishment of a flexible and non permanently standing force composed of all nations which would be summoned forth to prevent aggressions]. Since then there is nothing to stop nations. These permanent members of the Security Council have the power. They have a vested interest to dominate and not give the power to the UN." [Hence, no collective security.]

Back to October, 1985. "There has never been any real disarmament. There is too much economic and political interest in the arms race. The major powers and other governments in general practically never mention international security. The Committee on Disarmament operates on the basis of consensus and because there is no consensus it produces no results, and that finishes it. But if the question of disarmament went to the Security Council as it should under Article 26 of the Charter, then those who are obstructing disarmament would be unable to do so simply by not voting in favor, and then saying there is no consensus. That party would loath to expose the fact that it was against disarmament and international security by using the veto in the Security Council. The Security Council has never entered into disarmament matters; nor has it ever held a session with regard to disarmament." [Despite being called to do so in the Charter]

Ambassador Rossides devotes his time to bringing these questions to the General Assembly. It was the vision of the Charter's founders and was provided for in that Charter. No country can put down its' arms unless it feels a protection from aggression, and smaller nations now turn elsewhere for protection. It is in the realization of this United Nations force (which is in no way, shape, or form a world government as critics imply) that a basic security for all nations may be born, and a way out of escalating destruction may be entered upon.

The ambassador procedes, "I was present at a special gathering of eminent scientists of the United States and the Soviet Union. They expressly pronounced that a nuclear war is out of the question. From the very first blows of nuclear weapons the whole structure of the world would be changed.... There would be darkness, it would be hell, even with a few blows. Even if one side did not retaliate the other would soon perish from its' own effects. We, the small countries with a small voice, say "Listen to those scientists." Get rid of the idea of accumulating nuclear weapons. They cannot be used, so why spend billions of dollars on weapons that can never be used?"

Ambassador Rossides continues, "The Security Council discusses the quarrel between A and B country and they pass a resolution which is worthless because they have no means to enforce it. They have never entered upon the question of the arms race. Article 26 of the Charter says that the Security Council shall be responsible for plans for the establishment of a system for the regulation of armaments. Why haven't they done it? Because those who conduct the arms negotiations purportedly for arms control and disarmament, they are the same ones who carry forward the arms race. They say "We must see about negotiations." What negotiations? Those powers are the two responsible for the one and the other. The negotiations have been a stagnant pretense to deceive the people that something is being done about the arms race, which is a galloping reality."

At 91 years, the Ambassador is putting forth legislation to have the Security Council directly address the arms race, and then empower it to have the true effect intended, envisioned and called for by the founders of the United Nations; a realistic collective security for all. He is often a lone wolf with time, not energy, running short.

THE QUESTION OF UNITED NATIONS EFFECTIVENESS

"We the peoples of the United Nations determined to save succeeding generations from the scourge of war...for these ends... (agree) to unite our strength to maintain international peace and security....Armed force shall not be used save in the common interest."
From the Preamble of the Charter of the United Nations

On a one to one basis most all diplomats interviewed were sincere, intent and dedicated to achieving a more harmonious world, Since there are so many wars, so much tension between lands even within these halls, the question continually arising became: Where is the effectiveness failing?

One of the problems would be that the diplomats are here to serve their country's interests over the globe's interest. This mode of Thinking is slowly becoming outdated as we become more interdependent. However the attitude can be somewhat understandable in the light of natural competition when each country has its' own vital needs, and endless complexities to be faced with limited U.N. abilities and resources. When we include each sovereign state these needs and complexities are multiplied 160 times. For this fact alone, the great task, the wide ranging accomplishment of having over 160 nations actually sit down together at one time earns the UN deserved respect.

The UN Charter was ratified by all in resurrection from some of the worst levels of destruction, loss, grief, casualties, and inhuman conduct ever experienced by mankind. After

World War II the UN began with an aura of great hope and expectation. There was an air of good heartedness in view of the possibility of accomplishing its' noble aims. But the Cold War began and the essential organ of the UN for the international and collective security, the Security Council, was neglected except for in the words of the Charter. Now the institution itself requires it's own tight security, and the help of the New York City Police.

The tone has become much less spontaneous. The many daily speeches in the many rooms for the many committees, subcommittees and assemblies, have become carefully planned texts, refined and tailored to cover all angles like legal documents prepared for court. They are often filled with rhetoric and continual repetitions of a country's propaganda. There is a good amount of name calling, categorizing, scapegoating, labeling, 'right or wrong' sticking to blocs or special interest groups, and once again: repetition. Much of the communication does not seem genuine or direct, but full of now characteristic wordiness. One wonders how people can remain awake. The other unfortunate effect is that many simply do not listen. Everyone talks, but when their turn is over it is not uncommon for speakers to leave.

The secretaries seem the busiest. Everything is translated, documented, copied over and distributed. Most of the buildings are being filled with this mountainous amount of paper. Yes, the UN has become another hallmark of bureaucracy. It has perhaps the normal amount of unbalanced egos in places of authority but one wonders how they got there and why? Why in of all places the United Nations, with its high ideals, and where cooperation, service and mutual respect are of the highest importance. One witnesses the 'you do for me, I'll do for you,' and a speech behind the podium may not be at all what is said on the ground floor.

A world at peace does require constant communication, but spirit must return to the tone, and a balance of talking with listening recognized. Otherwise, as the great writer/teacher/theologian Thomas Merton said in his last address, "We cannot depend on institutions to do for us."

Although the UN is not yet perfected and its' actuality is still very young in the face of man's history, it is a beginning.

Some say a functioning United Nations is our one and only hope. No one strong nation can completely safeguard itself today, and it certainly cannot safeguard the world. The Cold War was not foreseen and the founders did not intend the veto power of the five permanent members of the Security Council to render the institution impotent, but it has, and needs to be amended.

There was a good reason the UN came to house itself in New York City and the United States. There is an affinity with the guiding lights of the U.S. Declaration of Independence and the Constitution. For over three hundred years immigrants from all nations have come here. Millions have passed the Statue of Liberty in its' harbor hoping for refuge, work, and the possibility of new life, a fair chance. There are few lands that would protect the safety of opposing and conflicting ideologies and allow them free communication and propagation. This is the only kind of soil a true United Nations can grow on and survive. The almost stifling decorum, cocktail parties, private limousines, and the sense of prestige and privilege are not to detract one from the spirit of the Lady in the harbor, the spirit of nurturance, care, freedom (with its great responsibility) and justice.

It has been said that if you want peace, you have to prepare for peace. It takes every bit and more the vitality and courage to maintain peace -- as it did in maintaining the wars of the past. If there is a next great war it will have nothing to do with courage, honor, or peoples' vitality. As Mr. Urguart, the UN Undersecretary General said, "Perhaps the UN was not meant to bring us to heaven, as much as to save us from hell.... There is no way the effort for a United Nations cannot be made. This effort has to be made."

Within the structure of the great assembly was placed a small and much less frequented meditation hall. In its stillness, it does not display the hundreds of man's symbols for his religions or philosophies. Inside rests only one large smooth piece of stone. With one small light touching it, it is as this planet journeying quietly through infinite space.

On the earth, the UN is the only complete sphere of contact between all nations. It is made up of individual people. Each have an effect of contributing to its' growth, or maintaining stasis, or violating its' purpose. Here is a rounding of some of the delegates' statements concerning the effectiveness, or lack of effectiveness of the UN:

"The UN's strength is it's political, diplomatic strength. Failure of the UN lies with the countries, not the charter.'" (from Cape Verde)

"In the UN things happen in block votes. The UN spends most of their time and money on propaganda against Israel and South Africa. The Arab Bloc supports the African Bloc against us (South Africa) as long as the African Bloc supports the Arab Bloc against Israel. It is pressuring and politics which have become institutionalized.

We (the nations) have moved far away from the Charter, which has been breached time and again by many. For protection, small countries need to align with a superpower.

The Soviet Union plays an effective role here in spreading it's influence; the price to pay for allowing opposing views. It is not the same case with the U.S. which pays 25% of the UN bill.

For nations there is an overriding self interest in international affairs, so peace may be possible." (from South Africa)

"I am optimistic about the UN. After five years here, I see the futility, but there is no other way. The effectiveness is really up to the member states." (from Czechoslovakia)

"The UN has been a disappointment so far. Everything is discussed, but there is no implementation by the Security Council. We are trying to change this abuse of the UN. We are putting forth another draft on Namibia. We'll see what happens after the report of the Secretary General about implementation." (from Angola)

"We wish for people to believe in the UN. It was established to serve the people at large, the people of the globe, and not just the superpowers. The UN is still the place to come to, to get together. There are many technical and educational activities of great help to people here." (from Egypt)

"The UN is the only place where the two ideologies meet. Multilateral relations are becoming more important than bilateral." (from Federal Republic of Germany)

"They just have an intellectual approach at the UN. You always have a little room here if every one would just utilize it." (from Chile)

"Human rights diplomacy is a kind of luxury. Our job is to defend our national interests. We wish to create an approach (to world peace). It is easy to lose sight." (from Australia)

"The major threat in the world and reflected in the UN is the growing tensions in the international climate." (from Poland)

"The superpowers are not interested in the UN becoming too powerful. In terms of economic and social benefits, yes, it effects us in many ways. Unicef, the World Health Organization and many other agencies do much good. Often their resources are reliant on private donors." (from Madagascar)

"The UN is not a world government. We can only do what we can. There have been many resolutions on the arms race, but until the U.S. and U.S.S.R. recognize them and take steps, there is no progress.
The lack of confidence in the UN has an unfavorable effect on the climate here. We see endless debates and resolutions passed with seemingly no effect, but it is very important when all countries can elaborate their position. World politics are reflected here, and there is credit to be given as a strong political field. It is a good forum for getting major politicans together. The whole cost of the UN is less

than one submarine. If a country feels it can solve it's conflict with another then it doesn't come to the UN. If they feel they can't solve it then they come here. As it is often insoluble, they then blame the UN.

There are other departments of the UN in health, social and technological fields which are little known and often not given credit. They assist developing countries in many aspects." (from Hungary)

"The UN is only capable of what it's members allow it to do. Governments and the UN may become obsolete if they don't allow people effective change." (from Brazil)

"The UN is a forum and arena. It is an instrument of international cooperation, and not a world government. It was born in the light of the great victory over our common enemy, Nazi fascism." (from U.S.S.R.)

"The UN wasn't effective for us in 1965. The Interamerican Force sent here was primarily U.S. Marines. But, the UN is economically helpful and the communication is great. The problems of the world would be worse without it." (from The Dominican Republic)

"Solutions won't come with just more meetings. We meet too much. We meet professionally but not with the spirit to get definite results. Resolutious don't bring food. We have to change the spirit of relations. It can often become quite negative. It is not black versus white. At the UN there can be a self intoxification of politicians, a separation between speech and reality. The UN is very important but it can often be a screen from reality. Diplomats can forget their original task. It is not a question of ideology, but survival. Reality will oppose us eventually. The propaganda and the rhetoric will have to go. I do feel a beginning, but just a beginning, of a new consciousness of and at the United Nations." (ffrom Algeria)

"In Lebanon thousands of people are dying. There is no progress. There has been a crystalization in the Cyprus conflict. No one is interested in changing. The United Nations Security Council is not being listened to because it is not a power." (from France)

"In violation of the United Nations Charter, signed by all, the Security Council has been deliberately denied effectiveness by the major powers. In 1946 they disagreed and have never tried to agree after that. They wanted to keep the force with themselves and not the UN. From here we have gone back to the parity of weapons, in violation of their own Charter to end the scourge of war and aggression by nations. The council passes well informed resolutions, but hasn't the force to back up it's decisions." (Ambassador Rossides of Cyprus)

Robert Muller, the Assistant Secretary General of the UN in charge of it's fortieth anniversary celebration has written this. "Each human crisis bears also the seeds of its own solution....So the world is desperate again and weary of all disarmament talk....and is looking for the voice in the desert who will help us out of the ordeal. The prophet is right in the midst of us and he's been present in the UN and it's disarmament debates for a long time. His name is Ambassador Zenon Rossides of Cyprus. I strongly believe that his time has come and his voice will be heard."

Ambassador Rossides has been emphatically pronouncing, "A closely interdependent world composed of many sovereign nations cannot possibly function towards peace, security and survival in a nuclear and space age without an effectively functioning organization. We have the United Nations; therefore we should see that it is restored to its effectiveness as required by the Charter, so that it can answer its primary purpose of ensuring international peace and security." His life is dedicated to restoring this effectiveness, particularly to it's vital and essential organ, the presently powerless Security Council.

The United Nations was not meant to be a power or authority over any nation or nations as governments have feared and propagated against it. This fear has stopped the formation of a security force which can stop aggressions and lawlessness and allow for negotiation and fair settlement.

There has been a problem of perception and old habits of control. The UN Security Force would not be a standing force or a permanent force. No one nation or group of nations could gain authority of the force. It would gather only to meet a specific need and disassembled when that need was completed. It would be assembled only after negotiations failed, and would be assembled with troops and materials only from nations not involved in the crisis. There would be no takeovers and no taking of sides.

The function of this force is to stop aggression and protect nations from overpowering threats. Terrorism and war break all the rules in the book. No nation can go against a world pooling together. When that is seen, the process of settlement of disputes can resume. The troops will return to their respective countries without "the spoils of war" but with the knowledge they have stood for a globe at peace. They too will know that their land can rest in such trust and safety. The cycle of national vengeance can come to an end. This concept is still in early evolution, but if there is to be survival we will witness its' rise to maturity some long prayed for, worked for, and millions-of-lives-sacrificed for day.

INSPIRATION

For the Diplomats

"Life is very short, and there is no time
for fussing and fighting, my friend.
I have always thought, that it's a crime....
We can work it out."
            The Beatles

"The real challenge for each of us
is to desire to evolve out of our fears....
There is no love or healing in fear.
Each person who lives in fear
contributres and helps support everyone else's fear,
until the struggle to live and love becomes more difficult
for all of us."
            Mrs. Ethel Lombardi

Each diplomat was asked where his/her source of inspiration came from to work for peace in the world. What inspired these people to give their time and energy to the cause of a United Nations? One said it was a job, many called upon God as the source. Most agreed that the United Nations Charter was an inspiring and guiding light. In addition to the above, here follow several comments:

"Our civil rights movement was inspired by the civil rights movement in the United States, especially for human rights. This effected me." (Ireland)

"Coming from a Moslem background I lived in Europe [mainly France] for ten years and made many close friends. Later I had to personally witness a massacre in my home town by the French. Having to reconcile this with my friendships taught me much.

Earlier I studied Heraclitus and Lao Tzu and was struck by some of the similarities in their philosophies even though they never met each others cultures." (Algeria)

"I was a headmaster in school. It got me working with the whole community. I didn't get into just more rules, but positive vigorous projects in theatre, music, sports, political debates, etc..

I keep in touch with the divine source, which looks down with pity and sorrow at much." (Antigua)

"I'm also a space lawyer. Space law is a new environment where peace must be reached. In my early education the concept of public service was deeply rooted. I worked for a small law firm but that didn't make me happy. I wanted to spread out to more people. Most inspiration comes from my family -- the most important cell in society." (Chile)

"Even though my generation did not start this, we have had a bad conscience about WW II. We don't wish it to ever happen again. (Federal Republic of Germany)

"Just being an Indian. Growing up in this ancient culture. Buddha was here 2500 years ago." (India)

"There are so many injustices that make me skeptical about my ideals. I am a Christian, which has helped mold my viewpoint." (Madagascar)

"Personally, I am involved in Indian philosophy; meditation and yoga." (Denmark)

"All my years in school. I did my thesis on the Middle East." (France)

"I was born in Angola but spent many years in Portugal until for political reasons we had to leave. I went to Switzerland where I made contacts with many different students. We were all messengers of our own countries. There are many things happening at the U.N." (Angola)

"The attitude of the Costa Rican people. You know, we have no military.... I've been at the U.N. a long time." (Costa Rica)

"I studied the French and German intellectuals who thought of an integrated Europe a hundred years ago. Now they are joining for space. Both my parents come from different backgrounds." (Brasil)

"From my family. They were involved in Christian community work. They lived in a way that is relevant to world affairs." (Australia)

"I belong to a collective, family and business. We are one people, homogeneous. I also enjoy baseball and English conversation." (Japan)

"I am a Christian Scientist. I do my practices in the morning and feel peaceful. To sleep soundly at night I give the problems to God." (Ghana)

"My whole educational approach was to see the reason behind what we are on the surface. There is not just one reason, and all reasons are interdependent. In any final analysis we must take into consideration all. We need firm conviction. There is a great need for global approach. Appreciate the individual and at the same time see him as a member of society." (Hungary)

"I grew up in a diplomatic family. We have never been colonized and have maintained our independence due to this diplomacy, not military force. (Thailand)

"From college, but the political questions have interested me and the United Nations is very unique." (U.S.S.R.)

"I didn't grow up with the inspiration of a UN but I've been here for many years and see that no problem can be solved in isolation.

The sociological society is always changing. Many of us are first generation born in Argentina. It is new and there are many viewpoints." (Argentina)

"I come from a political family background. I am a historian. That has been important. People need to read history." (Austria)

"My academic background made me think of the broad concept. I studied international relations. The broadening mental origin of our mind is happening more and more." (Nepal)

"God is the main Ideal. From there comes the world outlook and what one should do on every level of life." (Iran)

"My family were all victims of war. We experienced great humiliation. My personal inspiration cannot be separated from the inspiration of these people." (China)

"Personal inspiration? It comes when one see's people in very hard conditions, starving, and not getting anywhere. Belief in God is essential. Otherwise, the world would be very dangerous." (Bangladesh)

"We are in a region that was terribly shocked by the war. My family suffered alot for freedom. I was very impressed by the demonstration on June 12th (Anti-nuclear in New York). This is also the same feeling of my people." (Bulgaria)

"Inspiration flows from the belief that we are attempting something that hasn't been attempted before, a novel concept. I don't see anything better than that. It is changing all the time and can fail or succeed. There are continual talks. I don't believe in revolution which destroys. I'm a believer in the basic principle that there is room for all of us." (South Africa - one who is involved in reform.)

"One God. There are 200 different languages and customs here, yet harmony. Unity is in diversity." (Indonesia)

"We as humans and spiritual beings all have a common basis. Help people go into themselves. They then fit into the world more." (Togo)

SOME WORDS FROM EACH INTERVIEW

Candlin's Law

The period of ascent of a great power is marked by the ability to identify its enemies and to be much more dangerous to them than anyone else.

The period of consolidation of power is marked by the skillful maintenance of alliances and the maintenance of loyalty towards friends.

Decline begins when the power becomes more dangerous to its friends than to its foes.

The process accelerates rapidly and may become irrevocable when the power becomes more dangerous to itself than to either friends or foes.

A.H. Stanton Candlin

These interviews are arranged in the order of occurrence. They are not meant to be the official statements of a particular country, for those documentations are available to the public and each country could fill many volumes and shelves alone. Official statements are what you hear at the many meetings and often what you read in the press coverage.

What was attempted here was to get a more personal feeling of those behind the international mechanism and the decisions being made; an attempt to get behind some of the name calling, the rhetoric, as well as the true work of peace keeping. As you will see it was not always possible. Some stayed closely to their country's line, others didn't. Hence, the protection and privacy of "Representative from Ireland, Representative from Togo," etc., without the names alongside. You will recognize much of the material from use in earlier chapters.

All nations did not have "equal time", and many subjects were not touched upon. This was due most often to the diplomats' frequently tight schedules. It was my aim to keep to their words. Be aware that they have been given open platform here. My personal agreements or disagreements with

71

each person's view, each issue, each country's stand (and I have them) would make this an entirely different work. So this is deleted and left for your own good judgement.

Some facts will be outdated as political circumstances change constantly. What was said yesterday may be altered greatly by an action today. There was some paraphrasing as some interviews went well over an hour, and for most, English was a second language.

All countries could not be interviewed, either due to the unavailability of the missions or my own constraints of time, and not due to political outlook or realm of international influence. There were several nations' representatives not available for interviews but of some service by phone. They are not represented here, however were of value: Canada, Mexico, Cuba, Nicaragua, Bermuda, United Kingdom, Ethiopia, Sudan, Zaire, Chad, Botswana, Iraq, Lebanon, Portugal, Italy, Laos, Philippines, New Zealand.

These are not complete summaries of national thought. They are a taste of the thinking and the language of individual human beings from all corners of the globe. All were generous and sincere in their communication with the author.

The Representative from <u>Ghana</u>

I don't see peace as a passive concept. I don't see peace in the world now. There needs to be some changing economics about the exploitation of raw materials here.

Things would be better if the two superpowers would sit down together and communicate and not send statements at each other via news agencies. We were the first African nation to gain independence and had a visionary first president. He called for a united Africa to balance out the world powers, but there have been petty differences such as old colonial allegiances.

Personally, to sleep soundly I do my religious practices and give my problems to God.

The Representative from Indonesia
National and regional resilience is our defense. If people are happy, this is our greatest security. We don't want military bases. We don't want to be a battlefield. We are against nuclear arms and being an umbrella.

There is unity in diversity. In Indonesia there are more than 200 different languages and customs, and yet there is harmony. Each village has representatives who communicate and problem-solve.

We like independence. We join no blocs. If we join the East or the West then the other becomes our enemy.

The Representative from Togo
Peace? It's all in one's mind... It's realizing that we have a common basis.

Unfortunately, it often takes an important incident, which actually harms the flesh, to open people's eyes.

The U.S. is building resentment when they tell us how to control our raw materials. The U.S. fixes and controls prices. There is fear when the U.S. puffs it's chest.

Being real in the realm of politics is difficult. It means exposing yourself and allowing a vulnerability. People have stood up before. Many have been killed. People figure it is better safe and alive.

On a personal level spirituality is important although we must be careful not to go too far away in it. Helping people go into themselves helps them fit more into the world.

Every little thing we do affects the world.

The Representative from Turkey
Peace is very central to us. Everyone is biased by everyone. We are human, of course, we don't like or believe in building warheads, but...we have Russia and divisions of her Army on one border, then Iran and Iraq in a very unstable war on another, and Greece, our ancient enemy, with whom communication is still very difficult, on the other. Turkey is in the middle of a "theatre of war", surrounded.

Peace would mean having good neighbors, coexistence.

The Representative from **Bangladesh**

The present economic structuring is not in our favor. The price of our exports continue going down and the price of imports are going up. We then need more and more aid. We are poor, have a large amount of people and natural resources are low. Other peoples wish to keep their status quo. They don't wish to risk what they have to help us. If we could only convince them that in the long-run their quality of life will not worsen. Sometimes I feel people are at our throats.

We don't agree with the arms buildup. It only increases the tension, increases suspicion, and worst, consumes resources. We tend to only emphasize the others' negative side, and have no confidence in each others' good will. We must respect others' own internal affairs.

I am motivated in this work. I see people living a very hard life, starving and not getting anywhere. Belief in God is essential, otherwise the world would be very dangerous.

The Representative from **Brazil**

World peace? We don't define it, we feel it.

Media plays a tremendous role. What we have seen in the media deeply affects our consciousness, even if we're from the same place.

Yes, it involves constant patience, compromise all the time, moderation. We must realize that any decision made involves others.

I am for total disarmament. However, we almost had a civil war here in the 1960's and we not only import, but produce armaments. Nuclear disarmament is most important. Another problem is insurgency, which is economically based. What I see as the major problem is the deterioration of the language of politics.

I like to see the people taking power and effecting change. Governments, and the U.N., may be becoming obsolete. French and German intellectuals thought of an Integrated Europe over 100 years ago. Now there is a joint effort in Europe for space.

The Representative from Burma

As long as materialism is predominant it is most difficult to have peace. The economy for all developing countries is the major concern. We try to be self-sufficient and export/import very little. Politically we have followed a neutral policy.

The U.S. and Russia side together when there is a common policy at stake, like during the Budget Conference. They vote together against all the third world.

Politics is a give and take world. Once you are behind the podium you are bound to official policy, but the more personal contacts we make with members of other nations the smoother the communication.

The Representative from Austria

As long as this general climate of distrust continues I see many hard times ahead. The major problem is the deteriorating relationship between the two major powers. They don't communicate. We depend on dialogue between them. We urge and promote this dialogue. In our neutrality we feel pressures coming from both sides. We are, and were very close to the takeovers of Hungary in 1955 and Czechoslovakia in 1968.

The arms buildup is ridiculous. It doesn't lead to a balanced position when started in an unbalanced position.

We need to share our technologies with the third world.

We need to read more history.

The Representative from Columbia

For world peace we have to cooperate, respect others points of view and develop equitable trading. For the world we have to create a big, big movement [people for peace]. There needs to be freedom of the press and religion.

Countries need to know and talk to their neighbors if they are to have good relations.

Most don't see this arms buildup except the U.S. military industrialists and the Soviets. In both hemisphere's the common thoughts of the people are against this.

[Handing me a can of coffee] We don't just have drugs.

The Representative from Australia

Like most people, most Australians just care about their own lives and not international concerns.

Media of the U.S. and Europe imposes images upon the rest of the world. World news here [in the U.S.] goes for the juicy, violent or sexy images that strengthen myths under which the people seem to operate.

We are allies to the U.S., yet the U.S. is a great source of pain for me. It's a true great nation which elected someone who does not live up to it, who is not fitted. The country has many unusual and complicated demands on it. Its strong idealism can be at times self-deceiving.

If a country has more power, then it needs to be more sensitive, and not take it for granted.

Some less stable countries are resorting to war to generate a national unity. There is a lack of trust internationally and the rhetoric masks many issues. This heightening rhetoric is a threat to peace.

Human rights diplomacy is a kind of luxury. My job, as all the diplomats here, is to defend our own national interest.

World peace is something to aim for. It's easy to lose sight. We want to create an approach.

The Representative from Bulgaria

We're in a region that was terribly shocked by war. My family suffered alot from fascism. Russia liberated our country from the Nazis. We can now have some peace and we wish to preserve this peace.

Russia is misunderstood. We are thinking, real people, not just robots. We wish to develop exchange. The western press has to come to Bulgaria and see. We have no unemployment, free health care, and have now achieved an excellent ratio of child mortality.

Only those who suffer war really know. You must work very hard for peace. We are for disarmament. In the situation we have now, I think we are able to achieve an arms reduction. Your president, "Ike", warned of the self-interest of the military industrial complex. We are prepared for honest talks, without seeking superiority.

I was very impressed by the demonstration on June 12th [anti–nuclear in New York City]. This is also the same feeling of my people.

The Representative from <u>Costa Rica</u>

My country has been at peace. The nature is rich and our people have developed better than in many countries that have more. The human being will profit in it's own development. We have an affinity with the U.S. in that we are a democracy. Some people like to stay in power forever, not like here and the U.S. where there are elections every few years. We established free education in 1865. There is no capital punishment.

Cooperatives have been established; the import-export trade is not yet fair. I cannot understand why in this rich country [U.S.A.] there is so much need.

Armaments and balance of power? How? It never ends. Mistrust is the cause. We wish to help establish an atmosphere of trust and confidence. One way we do this is in giving out trust to the international mechanisms and international law, like the U.N. and the World Court. Since 1938 we have not had an army. We never had a strong military class.

The major problem today is the whole situation in Central America. We cannot be isolated from this problem. We want peace with our neighbors. We have had a few cases of terrorism lately. We have been criticized for not joining in militarily with other countries. In this point, we go our own way. There must be respect for human rights, and in Costa Rica people can peacefully protest. We have established a University of Peace.

The Representative from Bolivia

The same problems of the world are reflected in the problems of Bolivia; everyone wants control. People who have anything are afraid they'll lose it.

We are all the way down now, no money. The standard of living is down. We need help. We need opportunity to work. People must have work for a living. If the U.S. buys too much from the outside, the same economic problems can happen to them.

The Army backed down when the economy failed and they couldn't do anything about it. Since 1980 we've had a democracy but too many people want to be head. There are many parties without much education. We need order in most every realm. Work will bring order. We don't need foreign professionals -- just the training and the machinery. We have all the resources.

We allowed many Koreans to emigrate to help in the fields but they are now taking over many of the businesses. They keep to themselves and don't mix with us, so this has created more of a problem.

The Representative from China

We need peace. Only now do we have peace. We wish to develop and improve the livelihood of the people, without war.

Since the 19th century we have experienced war. There was the 1840 Opium War. We were attacked by Japan in 1894. There was civil war in 1920 and then an all-out invasion by Japan from 1931 to 1933. This was followed by another long civil war until the revolution succeeded in 1949. You can only imagine the damages. My family were all victims of war. We experienced great humiliation.

China is not a superpower. We are still backward and poor. We wish to develop good exchange.

The main threat to world peace is the hegemony of and the intense rivalry between the U.S. and the U.S.S.R.. Each continues to increase it's influence around the world and increase it's armaments in the name of protecting itself from the other and the name of safe-guarding world peace. Talks should decrease these results, but after each Geneva Conference armament production is increased. Each side says it needs to catch up. Be it in Vietnam or Afghanistan, Angola or Nicaragua, or the Middle East, etc., both sides deny being aggressors.

The U.N. should be strengthened.

[One sore point I neglected to discuss is China's take-over of Tibet.]

The Representative from <u>Denmark</u>

I find much of what happens here [U.N.] is done in the name of peace, but not necessarily from the source of peace, which is more metaphysical to me. There are gaps in income and there are gaps in understanding. It needs to happen on the personal level. Understanding must come to deeper levels. There is a lot of "BS" in official positions but we must work and support this plane too. I'm all for machinery. My first duty here is as an official. That's why they pay me. There are many different levels of functioning.

At the U.N. there is too much a language of condemnation. Often countries will accuse other countries just to gain support from others. It's quite a game. Peace can't happen until people outgrow and stop scrambling for their own personal interests.

The U.S. and U.S.S.R. conflict has gotten Europe more unified. Security has a more basic economic and social base and not simply a military one. We need to realize the extent of the problems on the earth. This total mass of problems may pull us together. Hopefully, this will bring the emergence of a collective objective.

The Representative from <u>Cape Verde</u>

Things are similar in all underdeveloped countries. There is a lack of industry, unemployment, financial constraints and little technology. In 1975 we became free from the colonial powers and they left us with nothing. We've been trying to develop a minimal infrastructure.

Because of the aggressiveness of the world system and fear of neighbors, developing countries need to spend money on arms. Development or arms, it is one or the other. You can't have both.

With much help from the U.N., decolonization has been big this end of the century. Any failure rests with the countries, not with the organization.

Nation states are a reality from the Middle Ages. I don't know if peace is achievable, but I see world peace as a large music concert. It's a question of global mentality.

The Representative from <u>Belgium</u>

We all say we are here for peace. The more [we are] involved, the ways to achieve peace become less evident. When I worked in a smaller office in Africa you could see more clearly the results of your work. Here the results can be of a very broad nature, possibly less tangible, but important and necessary.

Some people were astonished recently when we voted against a measure for the non-use of force, but this was for good legal and political reasons, and a new treaty may not be ratified by all. We already have the provisions completely agreed upon in the original U.N. Charter.

A major problem is the economic opposition of the north and south. The debt may cause a military threat. Developing countries know what they want. Developed countries' goals are not as clearly defined. We need to be flexible.

The Representative from <u>Angola</u>

Our problems are justifiable. We got independence. Everything -- houses and industries which were mostly built by our human and natural resources -- were destroyed by the Portuguese before they left.

We had no economic base. Yes, the Cubans are here for protection and the Soviets give us aid. We need the help, and we'll receive from anyone.

We have no real border and are in an undeclared war with South Africa. The war is ruining what economy there is, much being spent on our military. The solution as the U.N. calls for would be for Nambia to become independent. We have many Nambian refugees in our country and are being invaded by South Africa and their mercenaries under the name of routing "bases of guerilla warfare".

The Security Council of the U.N. is disappointing so far in that all is discussed but there has been no implementation of the decisions. We have a very small staff here and there are too many committees and meetings to attend, but we are trying to improve our contribution.

Presently it is not safe for an individual like you to travel to Angola. I feel things changing, and hopefully some day it will be different.

The Representative from Afghanistan

Peace is something relative. The expectation of war, moments when people prepare for war, is almost as bad as war for it puts a great burden on ordinary people. And with nuclear warheads why don't people see it as it is: a time bomb.

Our goals are to develop and build schools, dams, roads, irrigation systems, etc. The counter-revolutionaries["freedom fighters"] are against progress and try to destroy all these things. They want women back in veils, and some don't even want soap. Pakistan has developed sanctuaries and training camps and each of the mountain men are on payroll. The nomads are heavily armed by U.S. supported Pakistan and other countries. The border is uncontrollable.

We are not occupied by the Soviets. In 1979, we asked them to come in to help us. The moment Pakistan stops, their troops will leave.

We have a long history of tribal fighting. In 1818 there was civil war. We were subject to colonialism. In 1929 the government was overthrown and since then many tribes have never accepted the central leadership. They have their own laws and have been resistant to any reform through the years. It is the same people resisting us today.

We would like to be on more favorable terms with the U.S. if they would stop interfering.

[Outside in the streets a day after, there were hundreds of Afghans rallying. They tell stories of KGB torture, complete infiltration into and control of their government. They pleaded for U.S. and international support.]

The Representative from Antigua and Barbuda

Peace is a sense of justice, a sense of understanding that the resources of the world belong to all nations and not to any one.

We need an economic base and the developed nations should assist the underdeveloped in this. We could use help in developing the vast sea bed for resources, food and power not only for one state but all in the trade.

All global problems affect us and we need people to understand that we too are a vital part of their existence. The U.S. and U.S.S.R. will be isolated if they don't join in the third worlds development, and crusading spirit.

Yes, war is obsolete. There has to be a new state of mind. But how do you get a totalitarian regime to come to this when the dominant idea is mechanistic and the state is most important. It is, man, a tool of the state versus the state existing for man, as in democracies. The U.S. has tremendous potentials if its inconsistencies could be removed. The technology is here. It just needs the leadership and a directed will as with Kennedy and King. Their ideas permeated the world. Tensions arise with governments who do not put the people first. If Karl Marx put love and the human in the center of the machine it would have swept the world.

Nature is beautiful and self-perpetuating. If man can look at the vernal impulse and feel it in him, if he can look at the universe and ask, "Why are we here?" The answer cannot be for war, and to destroy each other.

Let's stop fooling around with dropping a coin in a hat and get down to business, to building industries and moving vigorously toward our idealism.

I have faith and hope, and am very optimistic that leaders will again come upon the scene and show the path.

The Representative from Dominica

There is too much turmoil in general, even within the family structure. Once a man has pressure on his mind he is liable to do almost anything now.

We are looking for labor-intensive light industries and a chance to sell our products. We are a good potential trading partner. The more people out of work, the more they are idle and the more problems arise. We are not experiencing problems with world peace because we don't interfere with others' internal affairs.

The Representative from Argentina

The global environment affects us all. We are not free of that. Each country has problems that must be addressed for we are all interdependent. World peace rests on global acceptance of global principles. Governments will have to listen, accept each others' differences, and develop a feeling of self-containment. After several years here I have learned that no problem can be solved in isolation. The limits of nation states are changing. Sovereignty is becoming more difficult to maintain. The world needs to continue to move toward a shared responsibility. This attitude is not unusual at the U.N..

Presently the framework of international relations is confrontation and intercontinental bribery. The superpowers want to have a say in all affairs. In terms of armament the two each have their own aims and neither is prepared to abandon them. We have good relations with both of them but would react negatively to either side if they put a hand on us.

Many of us are first generation born in Argentina. The sociological society is always changing. Things haven't been necessarily politically stable. We are now trying in our complexities to find a way to recover in democracy and seek solutions to reducing the internal tensions, mostly economic.

The Representative from <u>Chile</u>

It is very difficult to bridge the large gap between the developed and underdeveloped with peace because of the different political approaches and no one wanting to resign privileges. For me, my functions are to listen to others and to try and achieve the goal of common understanding.

The family is the most important cell in society. If the family is healthy so goes the society. It is frustrating because I don't feel the willingness from many here at the U.N. and the approach is too intellectual.

Space is the new environment where peace must be reached. Studies in Stockhobm have proven that most satellites have military purposes. Recently in Brazil there was a meeting of the Latin American Space Agency to help make this new impulse in space available to all countries.

There are many people working to build a new order in the world, a new world order.

Pessimism tends to do nothing, or just any old thing. I am optimistic.

[Since this interview there has been more coverage in the press of the protestations of people against the Pinochet dictatorship.]

The Representative from <u>Democratic Kampuchea</u> [Cambodia]

[More space is taken here to caution peoples. Here a nation, a wonderful culture and people have almost vanished in a few years of strong but misdirected idealism mixed with violent means, propaganda, fear, vengeance, youthful anarchy, and lack of regard for human life. Cambodia is not just a regional problem and we all must learn from the tremendous loss of life and order. In May 1983 I was urged by the diplomat to come to Kampuchea to help the west witness the present struggle and plight. A few days later I was begged not to come by some recently refuged here who said the border was very unsafe and there would be little to no chance of survival over the border. Although our topic was world peace, with this happening to his country there was only the absorption of survival.]

84

In 1845 Vietnam invaded and almost took over our country and now they are trying again. After the Geneva Convention in 1954, 2,000 Kampucheans went to Vietnam for communist party training. In 1960, Pol Pot began mobilizing secretly in Phnom Penh [Cambodia's capital]. During the 1960's, Vietnam troops needed to go into our country to fight the U.S. and they took this opportunity to set up and contact communist agents. In 1970, with U.S. aid, there was a coup d'etat of our government and Vietnam took again an opportunity to identify our struggle with their own. There became a strong communist movement here to help defeat U.S. imperialism and we accepted many more Vietnam troops inside. To exacerbate things and encourage us further, the U.S. in 1973 bombed Cambodia for 200 days and nights. Feeling strong in 1973, we refused to talk at the Paris agreements. We now recognize this as a big mistake.

We captured Phnom Penh 13 days before the Vietnam capture of Saigon in April, 1975. But we were being tricked for their communist agents had taken power of many strategic areas. After the liberation there was much confusion. We lacked communication. There were no newspapers or radio. The different communist groups had different policies. We worked the people too hard. There became much anger, avengeance, and much killing [several million of their own people executed]. We regret this deeply. [His eyes and body language affirmed his sorrow.]

In 1977 Vietnam launched an offensive and failed. In 1978, they went to the Soviet Union and signed a friendship treaty. From this they got military aid and by January 7, 1979, they had taken over our country and established a puppet government in Phnom Penh. This government now has over 300,000 Vietnamese troops in my country in the name of liberating us from Pol Pot. They are colonizing, bringing in many Vietnamese settlers and teaching Vietnamese in schools. They justify strikes into Thailand to follow us. Our struggle now is for national survival. We have dissolved the communist party and ideology since 1981 and see our wrongs. We wish to forget the past and be friends with the U.S., with the West. We need help. Please see what you can do.

85

The Representative from Iran

We are Moslems and see world peace from a monotheistic existence. When God's law is implemented, when there is justice in the world, there will be peace. Peace is our natural principle. War is the exception, the aberration. Passion, greed, and violence in the self are elements which are increasingly becoming institutionalized. Since the U.S. governments coup in 1953 they have been the main enemy, the main evil, imposing their view, economically, politically, and militarily. The propaganda has been, "For no reason these people have gone crazy, and they are against modernization."

We are now an independent government. The superpowers don't like it and hoped to destabilize the revolution. Since 1980 we have been at war with Iraq whose aggression is backed and supported by U.S. aided Saudi Arabia and Egypt, the Soviet Union, and France. King Hussein has bombed civilian populations, something we have not done, and he must be brought to trial for this before we can have talks. We will move slowly towards harmony with others when our people can expect human rights. We are harboring 2 million Afghan refugees.

We are not against the people of the U.S., but the government's policies. [There is an estimated total of one million people lost in the Iraq-Iran war up to 1985. Iran's main source of economic base, oil, is facing increased attacks. Great human atrocities are reported on both sides.]

The Representative from France

We are not only an old country but have fought a lot. We know we cannot exist without a policy of world peace. France is no longer a big or ambitious power. We have had to adapt to the world and change to a kind of nonaligned country. We have a very high sense of independence and believe the only way to exist is between the two superpowers. I don't know if they want peace. They can't have a huge war, so they have little wars using other countries. Detente between Russia, China and the U.S. is mostly pretext for each to fulfill their own aims and ambitions. The U.N. Security Council is not being listened to because it is not a power.

If you want peace you have to sit down and discuss, whether it's in Central America, the Middle East or elsewhere. I don't think Central America is an East-West conflict. It is primitive to say the Soviets want to invade this area. Their influence is a consequence. The truth is the people don't have means to live and are under dictatorships. U.S. citizens would not tolerate it. Treat people as you would treat your own.

We had warned Israel to act with moderation, abide by international law and don't align with colonial superpowers if you don't want problems. The Middle East is frightening. It seems only a war won by the Arabs can pull the situation out of deadlock. Ideology is a main problem here and throughout the world. Ideology is mostly pretext and you have to get through this bullshit to what is really happening. The conflicts could be solved quickly, but with the use of ideology, I'm pessimistic. Iran is undergoing a cultural revolution similar to ours in the 18th century. We are not angels. We have supplied Iraq with arms but not in a major way.

We are well armed and do not believe in unilateral disarmament.

The Representative from Japan

Peace is vitally important for we deal with the third world for raw materials. We are export oriented and depend on foreign countries to buy, which can cause friction. We have sometimes had to sacrifice our market for political reasons. Before the Iranian crisis we were dependent on their oil. This was painful. We are allies with the U.S..

Our language and customs are different. We do not speak often, but listen carefully. When we decide to cooperate on an issue we follow through with the commitments 100%.

The U.S. bases in Japan serve as a deterrent. The arms race is not ideal or liked but it is a matter of fact and valid, for there isn't an alternative now. Sweden proposed the concept of cooperation, but how? A climate of trust and confidence must precede this. Without this the reductions in armament cannot happen and are just idealistic propaganda.

How can we then promote trust? Only through actual deeds, not words. U.S.S.R. is in Afghanistan now. Central America I cannot presenly judge and understand very well. It is far away. We do consult with the U.S., our ally, when we think they are outside track..

We must take a step-by-step approach. Each country has a small role to play and needs to make a little contribution. It takes time, but with each contribution it all adds up eventually.

Ten years ago we were called a political dwarf.

The Representative from Nigeria

[Since this interview this government was overthrown by another military faction.]

Peace means having our own sovereign rights. We support all movements for national independence. Not only the Soviets, but the U.S. supports undemocratic dictators.

North-south dialogue, negotiations between the affluent and the poor will contribute to the solution. What happens in New York and Washington has a profound effect on all nations. The policies of the north, pricing of commodities affect us directly.

I'm pessimistic and think things will get worse. Aside from the maladjustment of trade and the global economic recession, there are overthrows of governments, ethnic battles, and many different loyalties to different colonizing countries.

The arms race is the third leg of the problem. The U.S. and the U.S.S.R. will have to work it out and if they don't, what will happen is too ghastly to contemplate.

Nigeria is doing OK comparatively and in Africa a general framework of economic cooperation is beginning to grow. We each wish to maintain the independence well fought for.

The Representative from Federal Republic of Germany [West]

Our problem? We are living on the border of two ideologies that oppose each other. Those ideologies are behind most the wars today.

Presently we have to be armed to achieve peace. We believe in the balance of nuclear arms. We live so close to the threat.

We are deploying missiles, but we want to be open with the Soviets and have each side show their maneuvers and armaments. The Russians won't allow this verification. We are trying to push forward confidence-building measures. The solution lies in keeping up the dialogue. The U.N. is one of the only places these two ideologies meet.

We have a deep belief in the North Atlantic Alliance. We can't face it alone. We have to be together.

No nation can live in isolation. It doesn't pay. We depend on each other economically, so we have to discuss and develop tolerance with each other. Multilateral relations are becoming more important than bilateral.

Even though it wasn't my generation, we have a bad conscience about starting World War II. We don't want any more countries or families divided by war. We don't wish it ever to happen again to anyone.

The Representative from German Democratic Republic [East]

We are for disarmament between the U.S. and U.S.S.R., and nuclear free zones. We are strongly for disarmament in Europe. Presently there are no means for verification. [Why not?]

In the Salt agreements the U.S. tried to get a better position. We need to discuss the whole framework. The U.S. has to find out they cannot change the balance and have military superiority. [And the USSR?] As a result the U.S.

89

is losing influence in Europe and losing more third world support. The dynamics in Africa are not the result of Russian development.

The Representative from Israel

Except Egypt, no one in the Middle East recognizes my right to breath. The aim is the destruction of Israel. It's a struggle for survival. We have no other choice but to live in our own country. There have been 3,000 years of prayer in and for Jerusalem.

My grandparents made the mistake of not taking Hitler's Mein Kampf seriously when it was written. Some of the resolutions in Damascus have the same wording. We won't repeat the mistake.

It is live and let live. Peace is giving me the opportunity to raise my children and I'll give you yours. As you can drive from Rome to Paris without getting shot, I would like us all to be able to drive from Cairo to Damascus.

We have declared a hundred times, "Let's sit down and negotiate", even without preconditions. I believe the people of Syria and Lebanon don't want war. The PLO groups are either extremes or super extremes. [Although discrimination of Arabs is quite visible in Israel]

We hope there is a solution. If France and Germany did it, then we can. If you had told me in 1976 that an Egyptian leader would come to us I would have called you crazy, but Sadat did. In April [1982] we gave 92% of the area around the Suez, won in the 1967 war, back to Egypt.

I do not believe the Soviets are out for it all but they have since 1967 cut relations with us and will not reopen them. They are in the background with the Syrians and see us as an extension of U.S. imperialism. We do not see it this way. We are, however, a democracy.

Lebanon was a most beautiful country, the Switzerland of the Middle East. It has suffered so, after many years of civil war and hundreds of thousands people killed. We want to bring our boys home immediately. [They have since.] We don't want to see any foreign forces in Lebanon. Many troops have come in under the pretext of being asked, then don't leave.

The Representative from Poland
For most other nations peace is an abstract term. Only a few countries know as well as we do the price of peace. We were the first nation of Nazi aggression. There was six years of occupation in which six million Poles were killed and executed. That was one-fifth of the population. There is no family that hasn't lost someone. 60 % of our wealth was destroyed by war.

War is first created in the minds of man, therefore Poland put forward the idea of the education of the young generation for peace. We introduced a plan for nuclear free zones in central Europe. We, as members of the Socialist Alliance put forth a number of proposals for the betterment of the international atmosphere. The major threat today is the growing tension in the international climate. The spiraling effect of the arms race is also extremely dangerous. Policies of gaining supremacy don't contribute. I won't mention names.

Peace means having conditions under which we can develop and ensure basic rights. [Western press and defectors are disputing the availability of some of these rights.]

The Representative from South Africa
Peace is an idealistic word and concept, which is used most often in a propagandistic way. My views of it are tempered by reality.

There is an overriding self interest in international affairs, so world peace may be a possibility. War is not in the self interest of a nation.

The UN has moved far away from it's charter, which is breached time and time again. The East and West are diametrically opposed and have major fundamental differences in approach. Every small country needs to be aligned with a superpower to survive and we are western oriented. It's democracy, freedom of the press, freedom of literary and artistic endeavors, allowances of expression of opposing views, and free enterprise, against the opposite, serving the state[And apartheid].

We feel ourselves to be a target of Soviet expansionism in Africa. The Soviet Union plays an effective role here in the UN. It is the price the U.S. pays for allowing opposing views. The U.S. is more often chastised. It not only built the UN but pays 25 % of it's yearly bill. The Soviet Union pays 11%.

We have been a scapegoat at the UN. The great atrocities of Kempuchea, and the Iran-Iraq War, etc. are ignored in comparison. The UN spends tremendous money and most of their time on propaganda against Israel and South Africa. Things happen here in bloc votes. We are outside from the African bloc so there is pressuring. The Arab group supports the African bloc as long as Africa supports the Arabs. These politics have become institutionalized. They all like to point their fingers at Europe and the U.S. when there is any collaboration with us. Look at Tanzania which has been the largest recipient of UN foreign aid. It has opted for an ineffective system in which food production and the GNP has continued to decline.

No one gives us the opportunity to forget any of our problems at any time. We are not the only country that has violations of human rights. There is definitely room for improvement in South Africa and we are actively doing something about it. Pretoria is scaling down and phasing out of white supremacy. The colonial constitution is something we long ago inherited from the English, and it is time for us to abandon much of it. We have been actively engaged in solving our problems and making constitutional changes, while the rest of Africa changes by going from one coup d'etat to the next. Each individual will have equal access in the decision making in this country in time. I'm optimistic and think we can sort out our difficulties.

It is not the same kind of conflict that existed between the blacks and whites in the U.S.. Issues aren't as easy as school integration. Here the blacks speak seventeen different languages and have different basic customs from one another.

There have been wars between blacks in the area for over 200 years. It is the industrialization after the war that brought people in contact with each other. Our forefathers came here for the same reasons at the same time as yours did (U.S.).

My inspiration flows from the belief that we are attempting something in South Africa that hasn't been attempted. We are working on a novel concept which is changing all the time. We need continual talks. I don't believe in revolution which merely destroys. I'm a believer in the basic principle that there is room for all of us. Growth is a painful process. [Internal violence and international pressures have been steadily mounting since this interview. Oppression of aparthied continues.]

The Representative from Spain

Peace? It's basically a condition of objectivity, an acceptance of reality and limitations, with room for improving. Things can't get much worse. We are condemned to agree. There is no refuge. We are witnessing the decline of old structures of control and don't know quite about their replacement. We fear it, but let's not hide it.

We were not allowed entry into the common market because of others interest, as with opposition by French farmers and the competition of crops. [Spain recently has entered]

We have a strong socialist party yet are members of NATO, the Western Alliance. We have good relations with the Soviets, but we have American bases. We are a western nation but have very old and special relations with South America and Arab nations. We've held negotiations with the El Salvador guerrillas as others won't. We recognize the Palestinian people and have more advanced relations with the Arab world than other European countries.

There is a long standing problem with England concerning negotiations on returning Gilbralta to us.

Spain was a vast empire before being a nation. We were a Church and Army barracks and left ourselves poor, for we have not industrialized.

[In the 1930's all the ideologies from around the globe met and fought in Spain's long, cruel civil war. The scars still run deep as no one was spared the misery. All lost someone. From a survivors mouth, a recent documentary summed up the one lesson learned, which applies to us all: "Do not judge others."]

The Representative from <u>India</u>
[From the country where a prince of peace, Buddha was born 2,500 years ago, hangs the portrait of another great human leader, Mahatma Gandhi.]

Peace is easy to say, but difficult to define. We have an ancient saying that helps. It is: "The world is a Family."

Gandhi's heart was broken when 40% of the Moslems created the separate state of Pakistan. Tolerance is an important extension of non violence. Peace doesn't flow out of the end of a barrel.

Imposed upon us are low wages and high tariffs. Non alignment does not mean neutrality. The 101 non aligned nations got together in New Delhi and joined in stating two major imperatives. First is disarmament which means no war and freezing of armament production. Deterrance is an illusion from the 19th century. Second is development, which stresses international cooperation and the restructuring of the world economic order. It cannot be done with attitudes of jealousy for it is in all our interest. The first south-south negotiations, the Economic Council of Developing Countries (ECDC), met for the first time in 1981. We are beginning to talk more with one another which is important but we need help from the World Bank which is controlled by the West. The only hope is global negotiations, north-south dialogue. There are some countries in desperate shape and need assistance immediately.

The Representative from <u>Egypt</u>
The permanent state of war for thirty years has deeply effected our budget. This along with the population growth has been our major economic concern. We've come from 20

million people in the 50's to 44 million now. So we are stretched for food, schools, transportation and social security. We are attempting family planning projects. We are trying to industrialize but we have been a agricultural culture. The desert is very good land if only water would come.

Now that we signed the peace treaty with Israel we can devote more essential activities to economic projects. We wish all the military budgets in the world could be directed to more beneficial humanitarian projects.

We helped establish and do believe in non alignment. Especially since signing with Israel we are accused often of being an extension of western policies in the middle east. This is not so. Our education is based on western ideas, but we are also African, have the Arab language, and are of Moslem faith.

The UN is still the place to get together. There are many technical activities of great help to people. It was established to serve the people at large of the globe, not only the superpowers. It's important for people to believe in the UN.

Peace has to do with being interested in living, with loving life.

The Representative from Greece

Peace is a time when people can associate with one another, work at resolving differences and not bring force into play.

We have several problems but see a threat from the east, Turkey. We feel they are constantly trying to get something from us and it isn't comfortable. They are making expansionist threats of the air and sea waters, and there are disputes over fortifying the islands between us. Both countries get military aid from the U.S. but we get $7.00 to Turkey's $10.00. We are a member of NATO and have asked them and the UN for a kind of guarantee of our borders.

In 1974 Turkey invaded Cyprus and now occupies 40% of the land with 15% of the people. At that time 103 countries voted in a resolution for the removal of their forces but still today we see the UN security force at the border and increasing Turkish settling.

To our north we have Bulgaria, Yugoslavia and Albania, but there are no real pressures from them. We are friendly. There is some anti-U.S. sentiment but only on specific policies, especially some of those in the past before the overthrow in 1974 when there was a U.S. backed dictatorship. We have four U.S. bases here.

The Prime Minister has asked for the abolishing of the arms race by both pacts. We don't have deterrents so there is not much we can do except keep the channels open. We've been following the north-south dialogue very carefully.

The Representative from Nepal

All is in here. [the October General Assembly Statement from Nepal]. It is better than my words. The chief problems are economic and we are one of 125 countries [called the group of 77] that gathered this year in Buenos Aires [The Declaration of Buenos Aires] and called for a new economic order.

A source of pressure is our population growth. There is also the resulting deforestation. We are friendly with our neighbors, China and India. We receive their assistance. Fortunately, we have never been under colonial rule.

The broadening of the mental origin of our minds is happening more and more. There is TV and other communications. People now are very informed. We like America. People in our land know where Florida is. You should come and see the mountains to feel our people.

The Representative from Czechoslovakia

Political and economic problems are always combined. We wish to develop trade and other exchanges but because we are politically linked with U.S.S.R., the U.S. won't negotiate with us. On a bilateral basis we have no problems with the U.S. and we hope to improve relations.

From 1618 to 1918 we were part of Austria-Hungary. We were the industrial area and produced the heavy machinery which was intensive in using energy and raw materials. Environment at that time was not important. This is now our problem for we lack material resources. We endeavor to change the structure and develop light industries such as glass, food processing and electronics. But we can't just close down the factories for people will be out of work.

Our gold was taken by the Nazi's and after the war went to France and the U.S.. After 20 years we've signed an agreement to get it back. Fortunately in Europe there has been peace since WW II, but peace has never been the general state in the world. There are constantly conflicts. What can be done is solving them and supporting certain international safeguards. We are against armament but globally the initiative lies with the U.S. and the U.S.S.R., more so than the UN. The real situation is very complicated and must be taken in completely. After my five years here (UN) I see the futility, but know of no other way.

The Representative from Algeria

We had a long colonization and then a long liberation war. For the past ten years we're focusing more on the economic problems of independence. Political independence means very little without economic independence. Since 1974 we have been involved in promoting international cooperation for a new economic order, one without domination or aggression. Only with solidarity with rich and poor nations, cooperation with all, can we avoid disaster. It is not a question of ideology now, but survival. The industrialized nations, the north, are not convinced of the concept of interdependence and that their destinies are linked with Mozambique, Togo, and so forth. It is not a question of optimism or pessimism. The world is completely different and we are all, Third World and industrialized nations, confronting several crises together. They are political, economic, and moral crisis. First, we will have to recognize this crisis, then we will have to see that no country can solve the crisis by itself. We speak often of war but sometimes forget it's reality. No one can be protected from war.

People are not looking for handouts or gifts. Presently the north-south dialogue needs developing. Disarmament is often a theoretical problem. In Africa the reality is food.

We are in confrontation with Morocco bilaterally now to help Western Sahara gain self determination. When the Spanish left their former colony, Western Sahara, in 1975, Morocco was fighting Mauritania over the territory and now has claimed it [Western Sahara] as theirs.

There is a separation between the speeches and the reality, a self intoxication by politicians. The UN is important but it becomes very negative, and often a screen from reality. Diplomats can forget the original task. Sometimes we are even conscious of this but do not believe in our capabilities. We meet too much. We meet professionally, but not with the spirit to get definite results. We often decide to mask communication by deciding to have yet another meeting. We can't have effective dialogue, or good educated postures if the reality is hidden. We have to change the spirit of relations, not black vs white. Reality will oppose us eventually, and the propaganda and rhetoric will have to go. I feel the beginning, but just the beginning, of a new consciousness of, and at the UN.

The Representative from Hungary

We are a small country and can't have a decisive influence in the world situation. We try to make our voice heard, and bear in mind our limitations. Our intention is to be as active as possible in cooperation with our neighbors. Peace is the best time and the best climate for cooperation. The present climate has an unfavorable effect.

Our goal is to build a socialist construction in Hungary. International tensions pull towards defense and away from construction. Hungary is connected by a thousand bonds to other countries. Half our income is realized through foreign trade. Most of this is with socialist neighbors but we have always maintained contact with capitalist countries. European countries are more ready, more interested in my country. We can supply a gas pipeline to them but their political alliance with NATO keeps such exchange from being allowed. We are more liberal but give support to the Soviets.

The East-West relations are a most important consideration for the international climate, and prevails. I don't like the phrase "super powers', but the two must have direct responsibility for developing world affairs. They have the political and economic advantage, and power. They have a direct effect on the whole. We can pass many resolutions on the arms race but until the U.S. and U.S.S.R. recognize them or take their own steps there can be no progress. One disadvantage is the manufacturing of arms in the military industrial complex of the U.S. which also has a profit motive.

There is a deliberate attempt by all developing countries to focus on East-West confrontation. The economic problem of the Third World is great and can be solved only with cooperation by all countries. Some say the capitalist system is best and some say the socialist. Whichever, they need to take active part in developing themselves.

At the UN we see endless debates and resolutions with seemingly no effect, however it is important and credit is to be given on the political field when all countries can elaborate their position. It is a good forum for getting major politicians together. It is not a world government. Many countries won't come to the UN with a conflict they think they can win or solve, but if they can't solve the conflict then they bring it in. As it is often insolvable, they then blame the UN. The other departments of the UN, i.e. Health and Social, are little known and given little credit but assist developing countries in many aspects.

The whole cost of the UN in a year is less than one of todays submarines.

A number of countries have gained independence with a socialist orientation. We need to let the world develop in a natural way. Everyone must have their own share.

My education and my approach is to try and see the reasons behind what we are one the surface. There is not one reason, and you find that all reasons are somehow interdependent. To know something well means to know the surroundings. It may be a method to study things alone, but no one can stop understanding at this stage. For the final analysis we must take into consideration all. We need firm conviction to do this. There is a great need for global approach. We must both appreciate people as individuals and see them as members of society.

The Representative from <u>Madagascar</u>

We are a member of OAU (African nations) and a member of the "77", the non-aligned. The five principles of the non-aligned are: 1. Non interference 2. Respect of national sovereignty 3. Peaceful co-existence 4. Non use of force 5. Against the politics of blocs. We have an open foreign policy. We will have tea with socialist as well as western countries.

Thirty countries are involved in declaring the Indian Ocean as a zone of peace. In reality we don't know if it can happen, but we are for the suppression of foreign forces in this ocean. There is the fight of influence between the superpowers and recently the United Kingdom sold the Chagos Archipelagoes Islands to the U.S. and not it's neighbor Mauritius. U.S. security?

We are also not comfortable with Vietnam in Kampuchea, or Russia in Afghanistan.

Economy is the major problem and the same problem for all developing countries. Our economy is in stagnation. If there isn't help in paying the extensive debts it will be the collapse of the monetary system. Developed countries owe the developing countries much.

The present tendency of the great powers is protectionaliam in terms of trade. Labor is cheaper here, and finished goods are cheaper there. There is competition, so they are not willing to help us develop industries. In the long run trade will only help both parties.

The UN is effective in many ways in terms of economic and social functions, as with the World Health Organization and Unicef. Much of those resources are reliant on private donors. I am christian which helps mold my viewpoint. There are so many injustices, that I'm at times skeptical of even those ideals.

The Representative from <u>Dominican Republic</u>

We are surrounded by other nations that don't have the same language or the same ideology. We feel more connected with the Latin countries of the continent, but they don't see us as belonging. We are not part of the non aligned. We are politically moderate in the Third World. We are observers, and feel like a contact, a mediating, country. We support mediation with Nicaragua. We think the major problem there is socio-economic, and take a neutral political position.

We wish to develop relations with other islands. We have opened embassies recently in Africa and Yugoslavia for cultural exchange. 80% of our income comes from sugar, but the price is below production cost. We wish to diversify work and strengthen international links. Everyday the economy is getting worse. There is a real devaluation. The black market is a strong group and is tolerated. Some families still own most of the power here.

Before 1965 there was a U.S. backed dictatorship. Then there was independence but fighting broke out between the left and rightist military. With U.S. help under the pretext of a communist takeover, the Right won. The peasants here are very conservative. Now the Dominican people are too highly politicized. There is a feeling of general discomfort. People are from the far right with a pro American image, or from the far left and want to take a stand as in Nicaragua.

There is a Haitian refugee problem here. Devalier tried to make a middle class but rushed people to wealth through corruption. It is a very poor country. The people come to cut sugar cane. Did you know that in the 30's Truhillo killed 35,000 Haitians on the border? There was no mention of this in the press anywhere.

The rightist view prevails in our UN delegation. It is delicate but we support and vote for either a Soviet or U.S. initiative when it comes to disarmament. The UN Security Council wasn't effective for us in the 1965 conflict, but it has been of help economically. The communication here is great. The problems of the world would be worse without it.

The Representative from <u>Vietnam</u>

Vietnam has been dominated for a thousand years by China, Japan, France and then by the U.S.A. invasion. We are small and we have to reconstruct our country. We want independence and liberty. We would like good relations with the U.S.A.. The war is still alive in the minds of the American people. The scars are still open. What were the reasons for the war? We know more now. The U.S. people cannot be confused or fooled as easily in Central America as a result.

We have had a duty to our half brothers in Cambodia to help them out of the massive genocidal regime of Pol Pot. We will not negotiate with him and the situation in Cambodia is irreversible. It is in the interest of peace throughout Asia.

China is supporting Pol Pots' fighting on the Thailand border. They assisted us in the fight against the U.S., but in 1979 they betrayed us and invaded Vietnam. They failed in one month. Do not trust the Chinese. China normalized relations with the U.S. to get into collusion with China over Vietnam. We have urged for better relations with China but they refuse dialogue.

We endear friendship with all in southeast Asia, i.e. Thailand and the Philippines. They do have a debt to us as they fought against us in the war, but we are ready to forget the debt. They share with us the experience and threat of Chinese expansionism.

We are on good terms with the Soviet Union. They supply us with many needs. We think they are sincere in their arms proposals. I know there are some business circles in the U.S. that have a big interest in the arms race. There is for them a great profit in selling billions worth in arms to the world. It is in selfish interests, and from the present administration I see no intention to stop it.

Opening up dialogue is the best and only way to obtain peace. We've seen that conflicts cannot be solved by war.

The Representative from The Union of The Soviet Socialist Republic (Russia)

We have a goal to create a new life since the Revolution. Peace is a most favorable goal. We are not looking for outward expansionism. [Afghanistan?] People don't talk of the U.S. as taking and occupying France, Italy, West Germany, etc. We once applied for NATO and were turned down.

The UN was born in the light of great victory over our common enemy, Nazi fascism. It is a forum and arena instrumental in international cooperation and collective security. In 1979 the General Assembly passed a resolution on defeating hegemony in international relations. We are for this and against the ideology of military supremacy. Our military budget is not profit oriented. We have not been the initiators of any new war technology. [?] We are ready for normal relations with the U.S.. Verification is misspoken. We do disagree with inspection on sight. In each General Session we introduce new measures for disarmament. Since 1957 we accepted the proposal to leave space open and free from armaments. We wish to prevent nuclear war, the greatest crime against humanity, and ban all chemical weapons.

[Most of the interview was often redirected by the representative towards citing U.S. wrong doings, U.S. weaponry, U.S. being the cause of much of world problems, and U.S. being responsible for the non-negotiations. "It is all documented", as is the opposing view of the U.S.. Stalemate.]

The Representative from Thailand

We have a reputation for receiving people, but when the cultivated land is being used for shelters it causes some internal social problems for us. Chinese refugees came here when they had their civil war. Over one million Laotians and Vietnamese came after the fall of Saigon, and hundreds of thousands of Cambodians have come to take refuge. We are a developing country with our own large population and can't handle all. The ratio of people being taken out by the

Australians, French and Americans is declining. There is fighting on the border and invasions under the excuse that we are "helping the rebels." Two hundred thousand Thai have also been displaced.

Vietnam occupying Cambodia to save them from Pol Pot is questionable. They dominated the communist party in Cambodia and Laos all these years and now we are seeing Vietnamese settlements throughout, the colonization process. The threat to Vietnam security has actually always been with China and not the Kampucheans. Pol Pot is Chinese supported because of being pro Peking. The Vietnamese and their Communist factions are pro Soviet, and supported by Russia. If Pol Pot were in control in Kampuchea he would be invading Vietnam, so they resolved to overthrow him. When they did in 1978, China invaded Vietnam from the north soon after. Vietnam is getting more tied to the Soviets. Hanoi is now in control, but no one will be able to claim full victory. It is largely a matter China and Soviets saving face. This conflict will decide how the whole region goes. The Chinese will not give up to break the Soviet hand with Vietnam.

We have outlawed either communist faction internally. Our people have seen many pour over the border with one atrocity and terror story after the other, from both sides. The people are disillusioned with the revolutionary governments. Promises have not been kept. Property and land has been taken and in Cambodia they say the new rulers are actually Vietnamese. The solution must be for the Cambodian peoples to rule themselves. The Vietnamese will need a government that is not threatening to them for this to ever happen.

Vietnam is the strongest power in the area. They tower over all of us, and have the fourth largest standing force in the world. They never scaled down after the war with the U.S. They could easily march into Bangkok. The number of Vietnamese forces in Cambodia alone are more than all our forces. We are trying to convince them that their economy is greatly suffering in such a state. Peace is the absence of war. We have not joined the non aligned. We have never been colonized.

We have maintained our independence through the years with diplomacy, not military force.

The Representative from Ireland

We are militarily neutral. We are not a member of NATO or any other military alliance. We were the first member state to vote for the nuclear freeze. We are involved in most Peace Keeping Forces of the UN; Our men are in Lebanon and Cyprus.

We were a colony of Britain for 700 years, until 1921. [Northern Ireland is still occupied.] We have the second lowest per capita income in Europe. Previously an agricultural society, in the past 20 years we have been campaigning to attract industries. Due to a worldwide recession there is 11% unemployment presently. We have a young and growing work force. Schooling is gearing towards technical skills.

In light of our experience we have supported decolonialization through-out the world. We make efforts to support traditional cultures rather than Western or Eastern influence. We are concerned about apartheid. We have a deep interest in Latin America and have provided large amounts of missionaries. A number were expelled from Chile because of working against injustice in the ghettos. We are concerned with human rights abuse. In Central America there is social upheaval and repression. The missionaries try to improve sanitation, housing, health care and the local economics.

Northern Ireland? [The history is too long and complicated to cover here completely.] British loyal protestants (Unionists) were sent over and planted there by England after a rebellion. Scottish farmers were imported too. The north developed industry and became strong economically and politically, but there always remained the strong Nationalist Catholics in the province. The civil rights movement was inspired by the U.S.A.'s civil rights movement, and in 1969 there began the resurgence of the IRA (Irish Republican Army). The Catholics tried getting even representation in Northern Ireland's parliament, but this was seen as a threat to the Unionists. The IRA now has two seats of the 17. With England supporting the Unionists they have not felt the need to negotiate with the IRA. England will not give up power unless it is 70% supported by Northern Ireland's Parliament.

The IRA sees us as selling out. The violent approach is rejected by our government and most people. Not supporting the United Kingdom in the Falkland Islands and the hunger strikes have effected negotiations, but we are trying to revise meetings with England. As we are geographically, we would like to see the country as one again someday. We do consent to do this with peaceful means.

The Representative from Cyprus, (H.E. Ambassador Zenon Rossides)

Beyond achievements of the human intellect, and there are many great achievements, it is the human spirit which will determine the fate of man on this planet. The nuclear weapon is an intellectual work. The Spirit of man can never go wrong. It is man's communion with the universal mind. Universal mind holds the universe in balance. Justice is not created by man. The sense of justice is inherent in the Spirit of man. If this Spirit is alive and prevails, man will survive and not destroy himself.

After many years of hard effort by many Cypriots (and without war) our day of independence in 1960 from the British should have been a great day. But it was saddened by Turkey immediately occupying part of the new nation. They have continued to settle and colonize what is now 40% of the Island. UN troops have guarded the border between us since 1960,

Cyprus has a history of civilization and culture extending back over four thousand years. I don't want security only for Cyprus. I want international security. My whole theme from the very first day of admission to the UN has been...[He reads from his first speech delivered in the UN, September 1960]..."We wish to see the United Nations influence increased.... We look forward to the time when an effective military force at the command of the UN will be a guarantee of peace and freedom in the world...We must look more wisely to the whole of which each of us forms an integral part, and on which each of our separate existences depends. In this spirit and with these aims and objectives in mind we take with gratitude and humility our seat in this assembly." (from International Security, Disarmament, And the Role of the United Nations, by Zenon G. Rossides, Agni Press, New York). The UN force called for in the charter is not a standing force. It would be comprised of all nations and organized only for the period of time the individual situation calls for, and only after careful deliberation and the passing of a resolution by the entire assembly of nations.

In violation of the United Nations Charter, signed by all, the security council has been deliberately denied effectiveness by the major powers (primarily France, U.S., U.S.S.R.). They proportedly disagreed on how much of a force they should give. In 1946 they disagreed, and never tried to agree after that. They wanted to keep the force with themselves and not the UN. From here we have gone back to the parity of weapons, in violation of their own Charter to end the scourge of war and aggression.

The council passes well informed resolutions, but hasn't the force to back up it's decisions. For instance, Turkey attacked Cyprus. We had a resolution unanimously adopted in the General Assembly calling on the withdrawal of the foreign troops and restoring peace and security in Cyprus. Turkey did nothing. Now, according to the Charter, then the Security Council should consider measures to enforce the decision. And to this end there must be force. That is the whole thing.

Take also the day when Iran captured the American diplomats. This is contrary to international law even before the UN. The U.S. also had a resolution passed unanimously by the General Assembly and the Security Council. Unanimous. There was also the same decision in the International Court of Justice. Iran did not care. They knew there was no enforcement action. They would not dare do such a thing if they knew the forces of the world would unite against them. So, here the UN becomes meaningless.

A closely interdependent world composed of many sovereign nations cannot possibly function towards peace, security and survival in a nuclear and space age without an effectively functioning organization. We have the United Nations; therefore we should see that it is restored to its effectiveness as required by the Charter, so that it can answer its primary purpose of ensuring international peace and security.

Disarmament is a negative concept. It means throwing arms away, and we cannot agree on parity. We can only be effective by focusing on a positive concept. International Security is a positive concept.

Article 26 of the Charter says that the Security Council shall be responsible for plans for the establishment of a system for the regulation of armaments; that is, towards disarmament. Why haven't they done it? Because those who conduct the arms negotiations, proportedly for arms control and disarmament, they are the same ones who carry forward the arms race. They have been responsible for one and the other. Thus far, the negotiations have been a stagnant pretense to make the people believe that something is being done about the arms race, a galloping reality.

(See also page 49 , and 60)

PARTING COMMENTS

"You know what I really think?
I think that one day the world will be great.
I really believe the world gonna be great one day."
Migrant rights leader, Cesar Chavez

"The superior man must always fix his eyes more closely
and directly on duty than does the ordinary man,
even though this behavior might make his behavior seem
petty to the outside world....
He is exceptionally conscientious in his actions....
Thus in his conduct the superior man gives preponderance
to reverence."
The ancient Chinese Book of Changes, I Ching
The Richard Wilhelm Translation
rendered into English by Cary F. Baynes

110

The Kor'an, the Torah, the Bible, the Gita, the Buddhist scriptures, and even existentialist works, all talk to us about a respect for life and not killing one another. Hatred not only effects the person or nation hated, but it also effects the person or nation who hates. It is personally and nationally debilitating and uses up our own vital energy and resources in the process.

Times have changed. Countries need each other, and not in the form of handouts. No matter how it seems in the beginning, it is a two way street. The idea isn't for those on top to go down and those on the bottom to rise above. It is for all of us to rise above our present limitations, for all of us to improve. There are such rich possibilities for us all creating a better life and evolving to places and relationships not yet even imagined.

Going directly to the basics: Studying a schoolyard playground of interculturally and interracially mixed children, ages five to six, they all managed to get along. They created games and played together freely. Yes, there were a few scuffles and fights but there was no pattern of conflict between white, brown, yellow or black. This learning and inculturation had not yet settled into their behavior.

We each should be rightfully proud of our own unique heritage, but now looking down from the moon we can see that we are not completely different. We in fact have a very strong common basis, both physically and as beings of spirit. The world is in a situation today where, as one diplomat put it, "it is not a question of ideology, but a question of survival."

We can do it. One of many examples: There are film clippings of thousands of Russian and American soldiers running across a wide field at the end of WW II. They dropped their guns, picked each other up, swirled around, laughed, cried, looked into each others eyes, embraced each other without knowing a word of each others language. We need to remember images like these and go forward to heal the political mistrust that developed soon after. The common people of both nations had nothing to do with this mistrust and want to steer away from the mutually assured destruction.

Nature reminds us that there is both a great beauty and unity in diversity. It also warns us in natural disasters. For during these moments all people forget their cultural, sociological, political, and economic differences and pool together for survival. The Greek roots of the word "disastor" means to be separated from ones' star. We are being asked to pool together before the very possible and unnatural disaster of nuclear attack, because there will be little to no survival after that. Even one bomb dropped destroys that much more of the earth, that much more a part of us. There are no longer strictly military targets. It is us, people, who are destroyed.

There is an ancient Chinese adage: Honor is given to the man (soldier) who kills, but greater honor goes to the man who heals.

It has been more than sufficiently proven that all peoples from around the globe can be valiant, courageous soldiers capable of offering their final and ultimate sacrifice; their complete life. We are called upon not to forget the lessons of these billions who have gone before us. With that respect,

112

we needn't continue testing our ability to destroy each other. There are other and greater experiments ahead of us.

In this one city of New York millions of people, all of us immigrants from one time or another and from every corner of the earth, daily commute to and from work. In most of these faces can be found the tremendous patience and humility acquired when dealing with all kinds, and needed to accomplish even the smallest of details. Not unlike people anywhere these are people toiling under the tensions, the pressures and burdens of the world to make the day work, and with the hope of a better life, giving their best.

If people were not of a basically good nature, no city or country could operate its' daily affairs. Diplomats, government officials and public servants everywhere owe their honor, and their livelihood to the common man. They need to remind themselves that it is their privilege, and great responsibility to be serving mankind.

The word disease means not to be easy; dis-at-ease. The thousands of issues flaming up around the world are like the sores exposed from a deeper disease. Bandaging the wounds is important but it is essential we address the core also, in which improving communication and establishing a collective security has a role. Our security is not just with the military, but lies more in an economic and sociological foundation, a foundation needing some restructuring and much attention.

As said by the diplomat of Algeria, "First we have to recognize the crises in general, then we have to understand that no country can solve the crisis by itself". It is healthy to foster the spirit of independence and self sufficiency, but no one person or country can live in isolation. There cannot be peace or world peace if each of us demand to hang on to all we have.

A fruit tree releases its fruit for the seeds to grow and multiply. A world of peace is not stagnant. It is a flexible one moving with the times and improving conditions. A content people is any lands' best defense. When there is suffering due to political or economic injustice, there lies the world's achilles's heel and another threat to peace for all of us. Many minds are ahead of our slow-moving bureaucratic structures. But we need the order and protection of law, and to this end we must continue with patience and applied diligence required in effectively updating and restructuring, where necessary, these bodies.

We have only recently entered the Age of Space. Already we are carrying our conflicts and wars into this realm, when we could be combining our efforts in the discovery of this infinite territory; infinite space, harnessing our energies for exploration of resources and opportunities to share.

The possibility of WW III is not too late to turn around. It is never too late to alter attitudes.

Peace is not only an outward smile but an inward smile. Not only outward words but corresponding good deeds; actions consistent with ideals. It's hard, challenging work. In this ever smaller world (from a telecommunications viewpoint) the adage passed through the millennia still applies: "Know Thyself." Many on earth have learned to bring peace into their own being, and this is where it often begins, for then it radiates out into all they do and towards those around them. This is most helpful. Each one of us makes a difference, beyond our limited knowledge and doubts and beyond what it seems, in all we say and do. Every thought counts, is registered, plays a part, and effects our world. None of us is perfect. We are in process and everyone can use encouragementt.

The earth is the home we share. It is here we give birth and grow. It is in this collective mind of individuals that the world is being saved. As did our noble forebearers, we own and carry forward the awesome responsibility, and honor, of becoming the futures' great ancestors.

The human race is at the threshold of a crucial evolutionary decision; a decision we never had to make before. There are three basic choices before us: 1. to become extinct. 2. to be like a conflicting and cancerous disease in the Universe 3. Or to live up to the beauty we can see looking back from space and be a multi-faceted center of growth and communication within the cosmos. No matter how long it takes, it is possible, because we believe it is possible.

SUPPLEMENT

From three Great Humanitarians

"Be ashamed to die until you have won some victory
for humanity."
Horace Mann

"Ask not what your country can do for you,
but what you can do for your country."

"Ich bin ein Berliner."
John F. Kennedy

His Holiness Tenzin Gyatso, The Fourteenth Dalai Lama of Tibet

This is from a man who knows the injury of having his land, culture and people taken from him, and yet has developed the strength to not give into despair or hatred. He withstood the many dangers and perils of mountainous escape and persuit along with his people. He comforts not only his people in exile but lends encouragement to everyone of every religious, racial, or national affiliation. Up to this day, with courage, vigourous stamina, clear conviction, and deeply felt compassion he champions for those who suffer throughout the globe. In one way or another that includes all of us. Here are just a few abstractions.

(With thanks to Wisdom Publications, London, for material from their A Human Approach to World Peace, c 1984, and Patola Publications, New York City, for use of "The Principle of Universal Responsibility", c 1979, both by the Dalai Lama.)

"During my travels abroad I have noticed many things which seem to differentiate West from East, and particularly Tibet. It is easy enough to understand these superficial differences in terms of the varying cultural, historical and geographical backgrounds which shape each particular way of life and pattern of behavior, but I feel that the far more relevant point to be stressed is the unity of these varying cultures and peoples. ...I always try to communicate with any "foreigner" I meet on the assumption that we are both simply human beings....

...Many difficulties arise frome ideological or even religious conflict, and men fight each other for means or methods, losing sight of their human ends and goals....

...When someone criticises and exposes our faults we are able to discover our problems and confront them. Thus is our enemy our greatest friend. He provides us with the needed test of inner strength, tolerance and respect for others....

I feel that our problems, though grave and complex, are within our own power to control and rectify. A direct confrontation with the universality of our pridicament, along with the ultimate unity of our needs and desires, is vital to our success. The need for simple man-to-man relationship is becoming increasingly urgent....

The noblest human qualities of honesty, sincerity, and a good heart will never result from money or be produced by machines. Only the mind itself can produce these attitudes. This mental development is not easy, nor can compassion be produced quickly. It requires brave and consistent adherence to truth even in the midst of dishonesty and competitive aggression. But it is the only viable approach for our future survival....

...The special quality of wisdom is essentially a human quality. To have compassion, honesty, and humility, and to regard anger, jealously and pride as the common enemy is to develope the noblest potential of the human race.

...We need to revive our humanitarian values....

...If at the beginning and end of our lives we depend upon others' kindness, why then in the middle should we not act kindly towards others?

Nations have no choice but to be concerned about the welfare of others, not so much because of their belief in humanity, but because it is in the mutual and long-term interest of all concerned.

...A variety of political systems and ideologies is desirable and accords with the variety of dispositions within the human community.

...The UN must become the instrument of world peace. This world body must be respected by all, for the UN is the only source of hope for the small oppressed nations and hence for the planet as a whole.

...I suggest that world leaders meet about once a year in a beautiful place without any business, just to get to know each other as human beings....

...We cannot create peace on paper. While advocating universal responsibility and universal brotherhood and sisterhood, the facts are that humanity is organized in separate entities in the form of national societies. Thus, in a realistic sense, I feel it is these societies that must act as the building-blocks for world peace.

...Politics devoid of ethics does not further human welfare, and life without morality reduces humans to the level of beasts. Politics is not axiomatically "dirty". Rather, the instruments of our political culture have distorted the high ideals and noble concepts meant to further human welfare.

...We need a revolution in our commitment to and practice of universal humanitarian values. ...It is not enough to make noisy calls to halt moral degeneration; we must do something about it. Since present-day governments do not shoulder such "religious" responsibilities, humanitarian and religious leaders must strengthen the existing civic, social, cultural, educational, and religious organizations to revive human and spiritual values.... We cannot wait for the next generation to make this change....

...We must live up to the same high standards of integrity and sacrifice that we ask of others.... There are two things important to keep in mind: Self examination and self-correction. We should constantly check our attitude toward others, examining ourselves carefully, and we should correct ourselves immediately when we find we are wrong.

...Developing a kind heart does not involve any of the sentimental religiousity normally associated with it. It is not just for people who believe in religion; it is for everyone, irrespective of race, religion, or political affiliation. It is for anybody who considers himself to be a member of the human family....

...Each religion has its own distinctive contributions to make, and each in its own way is suitable to a particular group of people as they understand life. The world needs them all.... The most important thing is to look at the purpose of religion and not at the details of theology or metaphsics, which can lead to mere intellectualism.... It is much more beneficial to try to implement in daily life the shared precepts for goodness taught by all religions rather that to argue about differences in approach.

...The common goal of all moral precepts laid down by the great teachers of humanity is unselfishness.... [They also contain] similar ideals of love, the same goal of benefiting humanity through spiritual practice, and the same effect of making their followers into better human beings.

...Anger is one of the most serious problems facing the world today.... Hatred and fighting cannot bring happiness to anyone, even to the winners of battles. Violence always produces misery and is thus essentially counter-productive.... Whether we will be able to achieve world peace or not, we have no choice but to work towards that goal. If our minds are dominated by anger, we will lose the best part of human intelligence -- wisdom, the ability to decide right and wrong.

...This is my own experience. When you are passing through a difficult period, if your mind is clear and stable, that difficult period is nothing but the best opportunity to gain more experience, more knowledge and greater inner strength. Future success depends entirely on present determination. Determination comes from hope. Without hope you can't have determination. Therefore, courage and hope are the very basis of future...."

Reverand Dr. Martin Luther King, Jr.

A man who risked his life on a daily basis for many years
in upholding truth and the ideals of a country he believed in
and loved. He had addressed and encouraged the United
Nations. Until his assasination on April 4th, 1968 at the age
of 39, Martin Luther King, Jr. was a true servant for the
people and vehicle of God's grace to mankind. One of
America's most eloquent spokesmen, dignified and nobel
citizens, his prophetic words inspired the world.

Leaving a foundation of concrete nonviolent actions and
his loving spirit, he continues to lead the way for us. In
many ways we are just beginning to know and hear him.
Continuing to ring clear are his books, tapes, and film footage
somewhat available in local libraries and much more
comprehensively offered at the Martin Luther King Center for
Non Violent Social Change, Atlanta, Ge., presided over by
his wife, Mrs. Coretta Scott King.

Here is a very scant personal selection, bearly touching
upon his panoramic scope.

(The following quotes are reprinted by permission of Joan Daves,
Copyright c 1958, 1963, 1964, 1967 By Martin Luther King, Jr. /
Copyright c 1960, 1968 Estate of Martin Luther King, Jr. / Copyright c
1964 by the Nobel Foundation. Selections from: The Words of Martin
Luther King, Jr., by ML King and selected by Coretta Scott King, and from
Strength to Love and "Drum Major Speech" by ML King.)

"Every nation is an heir of a vast treasury of ideas and
labor to whch both the living and the dead of all nations have
contributed.... Whether we realize it or not, each of us is
eternally "in the red". We are ever lasting debtors to known
and unknown men and women. We do not finish breakfast
without being dependent on more than half of the world...."

"...All men are caught in an inescapable network of
mutuality, tied in a single garment of destiny... I can never

be what I ought to be until you are what you ought to be, and you can never be what you ought to be until I am what I ought to be...."

"...If you want to be important --- wonderful. If you want to be recognized --- wonderful, If you want to be great --- wonderful. But recognize that 'he who is greatest among you shall be your servant'. ...Everybody can be great because everybody can serve. You don't need a college degree to serve.... You only need...a soul generated by love...."

"...Violence is immoral because it thrives on hatred rather than love. It destroys community and makes brotherhood impossible. It leaves society in monologue rather than dialogue. Violence ends by defeating itself. It creates bitterness in the survivors and brutality in the destroyers."

"...When I speak of love I am not speaking of some sentimental and weak response. I am speaking of that force which all of the great religions have seen as the supreme unifying principle of life...."

"...Moral principals have lost their distinctiveness. For modern man, absolute right and wrong are a matter of what the majority is doing...."

"I often wonder whether or not education is fulfilling its purpoe.... Even the press, the classroom, the platform, and the pulpit in many instances do not give us objective and unbiased truths. To save man from the morass of propaganda, in my opinion, is one of the chief aims of education. Education must enable one to sift and weigh evidence, to discern the true from the false, the real from the unreal, and the facts from the fiction.

The function of education, therefore, is to teach one to think intensively and to think critically. But education which stops with efficiency may prove the greatest menace to society. The most dangerous criminal may be the man gifted with reason but with no morals.

123

We must remember that intelligence is not enough. Intellegence plus character -- that is the goal of true education. The complete education gives one not only power of concentration but worthy objectives upon which to concentrate. The broad education will, therefore, transmit to one not only the accumulated knowledge of the race but also the accumulated experience of social living."

"...The emergency we now face is economic, and it is a desparate and worsening situation.... In our society it is murder, psychologically, to deprive a man of a job or an income. You are in substance saying to that man that he has no right to exist."

"....When an individual is no longer a true participant, when he no longer feels a sense of responsibility to his society, the content of democracy is emptied...."

"Human progress is neither automatic nor inevitable. Even a superficial look at history reveals that no social advance rolls in on the wheels of inevitablity. Every step toward the goal of justice requires sacrifice, suffering, and struggle; the tireless exertions and passionate concern of dedicated individuals...."

"I have the audacity to believe that peoples everywhere can have three meals a day for their bodies, education and culture for their minds, and dignity, equality, and freedom for their spirits. I believe that what self-centered men have torn down, other-centered men can build up."

"...In a day when vehicles hurtle through outer space and guided ballisic missiles carve highways of death through the stratosphere, no nation can claim victory in war."

"It is not enough to say, 'We must not wage war.' It is necessary to love peace and sacrifice for it. We must concentrate not merely on the eradication of war but on the affirmation of peace...."

"We will never have peace in the world until men everywhere recognize that ends are not cut off from means, because the means represent the ideal in the making, and the end in process..."

"Our cultural patterns are an amalgam of black and white. Our destinies are tied together. There is no sparate black path to power and fulfillment that does not have to intersect with white roots. Somewhere along the way the two must join together, black and white together, we shall overcome, and I still believe it."

An excerpt from Dr. King's last speech, April 3rd, 1968:
"...Let us rise up tonight with a greater readiness. Let us stand with a greater determination. And let us move on in these powerful days, these days of challenge, ... We have an opportunity to make a better nation. And I want to thank God, once more, for allowing me to be here with you.

I don't know what will happen now. We've some difficult days ahead. But it really doesn't matter to me now, because I've been to the mountain top. And I don't mind. Like anybody, I would like to live a long life; longevity has its place. But I'm not concerned about that now. I just want to do God's will. And He's allowed me to go up the mountain. And I've looked over. And I've seen the promised land. I may not get there with you. But I want you to know tonight that we as a people will get to the promised land. And I'm happy tonight, I'm not fearing any man. Mine eyes have seen the glory of the coming of the Lord."

Saint Francis of Assisi

Another man who revolutionized the spirit of his times through to ours. With his struggling, inspired and unselfish life being the true example, he wrote and lived this prayer eight hundred years ago.

"Lord make me an instrument of thy peace.
Where there is hatred,
    let me sow love;
Where there is injury,
    pardon;
Where there is doubt,
    faith;
Where there is despair,
    hope;
Where the is darkness,
    light;
Where there is sadness,
    joy;
Divine Master, grant that I may not so much seek
    to be consoled
as to console,
    to be understood
as to understand,
    to be loved
as to love.
For it is in giving that we recieve, it is in pardoning that we are pardoned, and it is in dying that we are born to eternal life."

About the Author

Anthony Donovan is the manager of the award-winning Keener Medical Clinic serving New York City's largest homeless shelter, and a consultant to organizations and hospitals in team-building, improving communication, problems solving, and navigating change. He was jailed three times for non-violent civil disobedience in Vietnam and civil rights causes. He's volunteered in foreign humanitarian rescue efforts since 1967, and for over a decade voluntarily facilitated and trained others in conflict resolution in prisons and mediation for organizations. In 1990 Anthony spent several months in the world's most-conflicted areas, including Israel/Palestine, South Africa, Northern Ireland and northern India, training and exchanging the tools of community rebuilding, conflict management, mediation and dialogue. He spent the following school year mentoring teachers and developing conflict resolution curricula for the city's most challenged classrooms. After working on a medic team at ground zero through the terrible night of 9/11, and recently returning from study at Israeli hospital ERs, he advises and presents on terror/disaster response and preparedness. He continues to initiate and support formation of Muslim/non Muslim dialogue.

In 1993 he interviewed an additional 30 UN ambassadors in a more specific and in-depth sequel to *World Peace?*, and is currently beginning interviews for the 2003, third decade edition.